THE CHICAGO HAYMARKET AFFAIR

THE CHICAGO HAYMARKET AFFAIR

• A GUIDE TO A LABOR RIGHTS MILESTONE •

JOSEPH ANTHONY RULLI

THE
History
PRESS

Published by The History Press
Charleston, SC
www.historypress.net

Copyright © 2016 by Joseph Anthony Rulli
All rights reserved

Front cover: Courtesy of the Chicago History Museum.
Back cover, top: Courtesy of the Chicago History Museum.
Back cover, bottom: Courtesy of Nathanael Filbert.

First published 2016

Manufactured in the United States

ISBN 978.1.46713.574.0

Library of Congress Control Number: 2016941438

We are like dwarfs set on the shoulders of giants, from which we can see more and further than they, not so much because of the keenness of our own sight or the magnitude of our own stature, but because we are sustained and raised up by their gigantic greatness.
—Bernard of Chartres (d. circa 1130)

CONTENTS

Contents

LIST OF PHOTOGRAPHS

LIST OF TABLES, DIAGRAM AND MAP

ACKNOWLEDGEMENTS

As in any work, written or otherwise, a person makes use of the toil, struggle and joy of those who have gone before. So it is with this piece presented here.

Firstly, I give heartfelt thanks to Felix and Catherine Rulli; Cathy, Bill, Michael and Samantha Kazmierczak; and Terri Rulli, with whom I've shared life. We are the progeny of immigrants from the nineteenth and twentieth centuries and the descendants of laborers since before the Caesars; we are who we are, in part, because of them. And by association, my gratitude goes to the people of northern Indiana, particularly South Bend, Mishawaka and Elkhart. We've been bathed in the rich racial and ethnic pool of "Michiana" and have received our work ethic there. I hope this book contributes to furthering pride in the journey made.

A writer is always indebted to those who teach mechanics and method but, more importantly, those who are able to instill a love for the craft. I was fortunate to have parents who sacrificed for my sisters' and my education as well as for a grandmother who planted my love of story and opera and history. I was blessed many times over in my foundational education at St. John the Baptist School and St. Joseph's High School in South Bend to have such stalwart teachers in all disciplines, but especially in social studies and English. My love of history, the written word and of words that I could someday write was nurtured at these institutions and at home, and (you should be thankful, too) I'm a better writer for all of them.

Also, my thanks go to the fine *esprit d'corps* in the Second City: to Bucky Halker, Stephanie Seawell and the members of the Illinois Labor History Society in Chicago, past and present—my most sincere gratitude for the encouragement, challenges and assistance given me. They've been a valued part of the creation of this book, and I cherish their work.

To the staff and supporters of the Chicago History Museum, especially in the Research Center there: Patrick Ashley and Gretchen Neidhardt, special thanks to Noel Dwyer, Michael Featherstone, Ellen Keith, Lesley Martin and Scott Ondercin, who were very attentive to me in my sometimes twice-a-week visits into the directories, microfilms and maps. Many thanks also to Jessica Herczeg-Konecny, Angela Hoover, Ron Solano and Sarah Yarrito in the Rights and Reproduction Department for their time, patience and good humor and to Joseph Campbell and Stephen Jensen for their work with the photographic archive. I give an abundance of thanks for their professionalism, dedication and passion for the preservation and exhibition of the good, the bad and the ugly of the greatest city in the world.

To everyone in Chicago who, in the course of walking around this place, I bumped into, bugged, bothered, dragged on the early tours or babbled on with the details of this work while in its birthing: their enthusiasm and curiosity have been infectious and spurred me on to complete the project.

A large amount of my gratitude is to the City of Chicago itself and all its connected services, particularly the Chicago Transit Authority. I have been a regular passenger of trains and buses ever since arriving here in the winter of 2006 and can say public transportation for me is second nature. The economic benefits to me, the ease of travel and my always-spicy fellow riders have allowed me to get to where I need to be in a timely (most of the time) and safe manner. This book would be a lot different, a lot less accurate and a lot duller had I not been able to go and check out sites firsthand whenever the whim struck.

And, by extension, to the Chicago Police Department—emphatic thanks for the risks taken daily for our safety and the efforts being made to work with communities in finding constructive solutions to our problems. In the midst of these all-important responsibilities, my thanks for the time given me in parts of this project.

To the Edgy Writers of the bimonthly workshops, my (almost) speechless gratitude for their honest input, critique and support in the fictional and nonfictional parts of my world. Their presence with me at our gatherings and at my individual readings and play performances, as well as our collaboration on the anthology project, hearten me constantly. And, by extension, my thanks go to the staff at Zanzibar Café and Nookies in Edgewater, without whom our meetings would be drier and a bit more tasteless.

To my financial and techno-teams in the digital and corporeal realms in bringing about the first incarnation of the book, originally called *The Working Class Smells…So Do Roses*—Nathanael Filbert, Katrina Willis, Nick Moutric, Landis Wiedner, Mark Willis, Kristina Zaremba, Connie Hansen and Connie Deuschel—my gratitude pours out for the selfless sharing of their gifts with me. Without that work, this book would be greatly impoverished.

To Hilary Parrish, senior editor, and the staff at The History Press for their belief in this project, I give special thanks, and among them a most heartfelt thanks to Ben Gibson, my commissioning editor, for his passion in the material, his attendance on my tour of the sites very early on as well as he and his wife attending the world premiere of the first stage production of one of my plays; and, most especially, for the guidance he has provided me in this heretofore uncharted territory. Another thank you goes to Michael Kinsella of Arcadia Publishing, whom I first queried about the project. After speaking on the phone with me, he put me in contact with Ben, and this is the result.

To one of my earliest fans and best friends—and the one most successful at keeping me from ever possessing anything close to an over-inflated sense of self—my thanks go to Austin Black.

To my co-workers and management at Trader Joe's on Clybourn Avenue, my day-in, day-out companions in this life we're sharing—they make a potential drudgery a true joy. Also thanks to the Trader Joe's Company, which has given me employment and the financial security for almost a decade, enabling me the luxury of time to complete this book.

A heartfelt thanks also to my comrades in the Socialist, Anarchist and Communist camps: their passionate and peaceful presence in the city from the Occupy events to the annual May Day, teachers' and protest rallies proves that Liberty still has a voice, and it's not the one piped through the Mainstream.

Lastly, and most passionately, I thank all those workers of our past upon whose shoulders we've been supported. Their blood, sweat and tears have reaped a harvest of a more just workplace than was known a century and a half ago. Though we've not come as far as some had hoped, we have come further than many had dreamed because of them.

LIBERTY, EQUALITY, FRATERNITY TO ALL!

The Haymarket Scoop
in a Nutshell

O n May 4, 1886, in the first days of a nationwide strike for the eight-hour workday, a dynamite bomb was thrown into a police phalanx in the final minutes of a labor protest meeting on Chicago's near west side, today's West Loop neighborhood. For the murder of Officer Mathias Degan, the first of eight police officers to die in the bombing, eight men were brought to trial and found guilty: Albert Parsons, August Spies, Adolph Fischer and George Engel were hanged; Louis Lingg committed suicide the day before the execution; Samuel Fielden and Michael Schwab, after requesting it, received commuted life sentences; and Oscar Neebe received fifteen years of hard labor. Fielden, Schwab and Neebe were later pardoned by Governor John Peter Altgeld in 1893 and released.

The bombing and the events flowing from it, the "Haymarket Affair," are not widely known. These events of almost a century and a half ago have had far-reaching consequences into the present century just as they had causes stretching back the decades before them. While not a detailed or definitive history, this book lays out a general path for clearer understanding and includes a study of the major sites in Chicago related to the events at the Haymarket.

By reading about and possibly visiting the sites herein, I hope you will gain a better sense of our history: what was won, lost and still remains to be accomplished in the struggle for economic security, improved conditions in the workplace, a more equitable distribution of the fruits

The Haymarket condemned. *Courtesy of the Chicago History Museum.*

Entered according to Act of Congress in the year 1887, by PAUL J. MORAND, in the Office of the Librarian of Congress, at Washington.

PRINCIPALS IN THE HAYMARKET RIOT,

Chicago, 1886.

| GEO. INGHAM,
Attorney. | JULIUS S. GRINNELL,
State's Attorney. | Judge JOS. E. GARY. | Capt. WM. P. BLACK,
Attorney | WM. A. FOSTER,
Attorney. |

Capt. WM. BUCKLEY   Capt. MICHAEL SCHAACK. FREDRICK EBERSOLD,   JOHN BONFIELD,   Capt. WM. WARD.
Capt. A. W. HATHAWAY.   Chief of Police.   Inspector of Police   Capt. SIMON O'DONNELL.

ALB'T R. PARSONS   AUG. SPIES.   LOUIS LINGG.   SAM'L FIELDEN.   ADOLPH FISCHER.   MICH'L SCHWAB.   GEO. ENGEL.   OSCAR W. NEEBE.

The principal players. *Courtesy of the Chicago History Museum.*

of labor that has been and still is out of reach for so many around the world and the peaceful coexistence of all peoples. Finally, in the midst of all the presented material, I hope that you'll gain satisfaction in knowing a little more about the fascinating history of this fascinating city.

CHAPTER 1

LET'S GET ONE THING STRAIGHT

M y third grade teacher, Sister Consortia, of the Order of St. Francis, provided me (unbeknownst to her and not realized by me until four decades later) with an appropriate metaphor for the premise of this book. While, yes, it is a book about the Haymarket Affair and the sites connected to it, it's going to be, I hope, a very beneficial exercise in "rubber necking." In our classroom, anyone caught looking around, gawking at something that was none of their business while she was speaking or while one should have been doing desk work would be singled out: "X! Quit your rubber necking!" And she would move on. Well, she will forgive me for engaging in such *verboten* activity.

The objective study of history necessitates a certain amount of rubber necking—stretching ourselves so that we can get a better look at what was happening at a particular time and place, poking around in areas that might not necessarily seem to be in our purview. The historian needs to be a snoop. He or she needs to get the nose where it doesn't naturally go. The goal is to have a better record of the human story and to remind ourselves of that story.

There's the saying from George Santayana, published in 1905, where he claims that "those who cannot remember the past are condemned to repeat it." The furtherance of the thought is that those who can remember the past are condemned to watch those ignorant of history repeat it. And so we have the human experience here and now, almost two decades deep into the twenty-first century. We have this knack for seeing ourselves, our times, our experiences as unique to us, and this clouds our ability to creatively think through effective solutions to some of the most gripping problems we face.

It was said in 2001 that the attacks on September 11 changed the world. In a sense it was true: the list of nations touched firsthand by international terrorism got one of its largest members ever. By the explosions, dust and blood at the World Trade Center, the Pentagon and around Shanksville, Pennsylvania, the United States was initiated into a club that was becoming less and less exclusive. The worldwide fight against organized chaos would never be the same.

However, at the same time, "9/11" changed mainly the North American perception of terrorism; a large portion of the world had been experiencing such acts for decades throughout the nineteenth and twentieth centuries. It was only in late 2001 that it was stepped up on a personal level in the United States.

It's good to remember, though, that even here we had not been free from this type of violence. One need only recall the 1995 bombing of the Murrah Federal Building in Oklahoma City, the first World Trade Center bombing in 1993, the string of shootings at U.S. post offices by postal workers since 1983 (from which the term "going postal" originated), the countless acts of gang violence from the vintage Mafia days to the present blood feuds running from Bogotá to all points North American. All highlight the tragedy of the human experience of violence at the hands of anyone with an agenda and the money, power and will to sacrifice others for it.

Added to this mix in our day are the horrifying experiences of a largely young, African American, male population and the police. Too often for our comfort have news outlets shined a light on the brutality of the urban scene, the conflict between citizens (criminals and non-criminals) and officers (law-abiding and law-breaking) that blurs the line between civic safeguarding and outright military engagement. With a waterfall-like abundance of armaments available to the lawless element, law enforcement seems to have taken on the dystopian view of safety-at-all-costs that has led to an apparent nationwide "shoot to kill" command to reinstate civil order.

Our present circumstance of unrest is not unique to history. While racial prejudice and tensions have existed for far too long, social tensions in general have ample examples for us. In this city alone, through the 1968 protests/riots after Martin Luther King's assassination and at the Democratic Convention, the 1919 race riots, the numerous "Red Scares" since the late nineteenth century, we can see fuses of all types being laid down, lit and exploding. Roots of these tendencies can be traced back nationwide to the first major case of drawn blood in this country: the protests that led to the British military firing on colonists in Boston in 1770.

The Haymarket bombing in Chicago on May 4, 1886—the first civilian bombing in the United States—smeared the face of the American public with a blood that would not easily wipe off. For some, it was to serve as the battle cry of a new life for the working class in the city, the nation and the world; but it left others in the city, country and across the globe frightened and suspicious of liberty and equality, ever-cautious about the reality of human fraternity—two very different perspectives.

All actions and inactions have consequences, and sometimes these consequences are experienced for years and generations afterward, as in places like Ireland, South Africa and the "Holy Land." The events of May 4 over 130 years ago have affected how most Americans view Socialism,[1] May Day and, to a certain point, the labor movement and social reform.

The cultural scene wasn't always suspicious of reform. This book will explore in a cursory fashion the events that occurred and changed the attitudes of the typical American citizen to support the capitalist power structure of the Industrial Age, keeping quite a distance from Socialistic principles, even when these principles upheld basic protections to the worker and consumer against unjust wages, exorbitant industrial profit and rising consumer prices. The causes of this shift came relatively quickly; from the time of the Civil War until the bomb was thrown in 1886, one generation, the security of industry was assured and labor had to wait until the shadows of the Second World War encroached to reap somewhat of the harvest sown over fifty years prior.

Upton Sinclair's *The Jungle* was intended by the author as a Socialist manifesto in 1906—much more down to earth than Karl Marx's *Communist Manifesto*. But the novel doesn't have its high status in the realm of American literature for this reason. Through the story of a struggling Lithuanian family, Sinclair unintentionally exposed the horribly unsanitary conditions of the food production industry at the turn of the century. We as a people couldn't tolerate a Socialist muckraker, so we sanitized him and heaped accolades on him, grateful for the part he played in the eventual creation of the Food and Drug Administration. Similarly, Eugene Debs is the only Socialist presidential candidate to tally significant votes (6 percent of the total votes cast, almost one million votes, in the 1912 election), but even at the writing of this book, Bernie Sanders (whether he wins or not) wouldn't be anywhere near the level he presently has reached close to the end of the primaries had he run as a Socialist.

There is something intolerable to the psyche of this country concerning this political philosophy, and its roots predate the Haymarket bombing. Violence, subversion, confiscation of property, suppression of worker incentive and totalitarianism (thanks, Uncle Joe Stalin!) are all brought out as evidence against it. And the same reasoning has led to the American celebration of Labor Day in September rather than on May 1. Distance from anything approaching radicalism has been accepted as a cultural value, and it's important to explore how it came about and why it's still this way.

Again, we are who we are as a people because we are who we are as individuals. Individuals are hopeful, proud, loving, fearful, vengeful, petty; we possess a long memory for resentment and are probably too amnesiac for our own good when it comes to root causes of things. As individuals we make up "a people." We as individuals make up a society, national attitudes and cultural mores—everything we mean when we talk about the clump of human beings in a particular place at a specific time. I hope that this work is like a mirror in addition to a brief history—less a gavel of judgment and more a bench upon which to stand and look out as well as to sit and reflect. Reflection is a fading art, but for a people to survive more than simply in a day-to-day fashion, that people needs to pause and contemplate higher realms—the places that exist above food courts, movie theaters and sports arenas.

Equally true, we need to admit the reality that events are perceived through less than 20/20 vision. All history is told, whether firsthand or not, through flawed human interpretation, tainted by some ignorance and more-than-we'd-like-to-admit personal biases. We remember specific things about specific events, but so does everyone else. Each of our filters are different, and those differences add color to the telling of stories—a great asset for creating a narrative but a little vexing for news reporting and history writing. This point cannot be overly stressed. Because of our limited ability to remember exactly or in total objectivity, it remains so important to understand past events by studying them more carefully.

As individuals who interact with other individuals daily, face to face or in the electronic sphere, we have an obligation to get at facts. The classic rumor mill that has never experienced a work stoppage and the simplistic acceptance of stories posted online that spreads like the stink of a backed up sewer pipe show that we have so far to go before we can reach the level of "doing" good history.

By studying history in general and a particular moment in the past, one becomes better able to understand circumstances here and now. If we can take an event such as the Haymarket Affair and study it as objectively as possible, we may be able to understand our situation today better. Where did the main players of the trial follow the law or follow their passion or fear? And how do we, today, behave in similar ways? If one of the hot button issues today is police brutality, then we could study the past, particularly in Chicago, and bring history to bear on our present needs. For example, it does no one any good to say that this city's problems of institutionalized racism and police violence go back a half century; the record is clear that suspicion of and violence against foreigners and outsiders of all stripes and skin tones have been among some of the few consistencies in this city almost since its founding. And in fairness, it must be admitted that it's of little help to finger point, to blame with no constructive alternative plan. Protest for its own sake doesn't raise anyone to a better situation, but rallying for a cause, with alternative propositions presented—even presented loudly—is much more faithful to the greater cause of liberty and human progress.

Tensions among a people have always been and will be with us as long as two or more people hang around each other for any length of time. Solutions come with greater understanding. This work shows that the instances of civil strife, which predate the War Between the States, rose in Chicago and very rarely were met with anything but ignorance, fear and their best-known offspring, hatred and violence. No amount of hiding from, discoloring or distorting what actually happened in the past can make our present problems any better. It would be the same for a doctor examining a patient and seeing the family history of breast cancer: the physician's denial of the preponderance of the disease in a particular family won't cause the cancer to not appear or automatically go into remission or do anything but what it will do. The study of history has to be as honest and courageous as a doctor and patient in such a situation.

In our present day, we have access to as complete an archive of the documented material of the Haymarket bombing, jury selection, trial proceedings, initial judgment, appeals and final judgment as we most likely will ever be able to find. The digitized trial transcripts allow students and historians anywhere in the world easy access to invaluable primary source material. And, since 2011, more light has been spread out over the whole story in a more even manner. The first historian to utilize these digital files in their totality, Timothy Messer-Kruse, has enabled those who follow (me included) a clear path to this more evenly dispersed light of historical truth.

In what has been traditionally seen as an illegal trial with a biased judge, an out-for-blood prosecuting attorney against a black banner–waving, crusade-fighting defense team isn't so clear cut anymore. According to the transcripts and Messer-Kruse's research into late nineteenth-century Illinois law, the investigation and trial were carried out in scrupulous detail.

However, it does need to be stated emphatically over and over again that state and federal law concerning strikes, rallies, public speech, the property-less class, police tactics, searches and seizures, arrests, conspiracy charges and all the other points on which the Haymarket Affair touches were consistently found to favor individuals and corporations of wealth and political power and the general defenders of structure and order in society's life.[2]

To put it briefly, the state, through Prosecutor Julius Grinnell and Judge Joseph Gary, reacted in the only way possible to ensure the status quo—that things (life, work, power) remained the same. In fairness, though, the defense team of William Black, Moses Solomon, Sigmund Zeisler and William Foster was inexperienced in a trial for a capital crime. Some of their mistakes were catastrophic for the eight accused. The attorneys could have requested separate trials for their clients, and most likely, Parsons and Spies would have been spared the scaffold.

The defense was supportive of the bailiff, Henry L. Ryce, chosen to go out and find potential jurors to question.[3] A reading of the *Chicago Daily Tribune* on the day after jury selection had been completed shows the list of the twelve empanelled. Most of the men were low-level company employees, salesmen or self-employed. Not one would be seen then or now as wealthy—but also, to keep the balance, none of them was at all sympathetic to the cause of Socialism or Anarchism either.[4]

So this leaves us with quite the task and not a little more responsibility to get at facts that aren't as easily attainable as simply keying in a word for an online search. Accessible as the information is, it still requires sifting through and applying our rational capacity in order to interpret events, sometimes judge historical personages and oftentimes reevaluate preconceived notions of past events. We cannot be satisfied with a smug Facebook-style posting of bumper sticker wisdom that supports one position and ridicules those who think differently, waddling in bigotry with intolerance sticking to us like sludge from a swamp. This is the kind of behavior that over the past several years has led to our inability to debate real issues (or really to debate at all), and we have ended up with presidential candidates talking at, yelling at, sniping at one another in the gutter style of *The Jerry Springer Show* rather than reaching the heights of the Olympian-like philosophy of Plato's *Republic*.

The best way out of the muck is to first reach up and climb from the pit, then towel off and begin the further ascent to something better, more dignified, more respectful, more hopeful. The historical record and our own rational, human capacity to think are our ladders and clean linen. We can wash ourselves in the bath of a truth that's already accessible to us. We have merely to think, to use that one single capacity that among all the rest differentiates us from our fellow creatures on this planet. To answer probing questions is a great gift that becomes only possible with our reason.

What are the similarities and differences today as compared to the labor scene in post–Civil War industrialized Chicago? And what can these teach us about contemporary challenges—from state-sponsored terrorism, to "active shooters" in schools and workplaces, to urban unrest, to labor issues today? How can we best assess past events and have them help us to honestly converse with one another about solutions today?

This work seeks to explore these questions through an outline of the Haymarket Affair and an exploration of related sites in the city in the hopes of shedding light on our contemporary situation for the benefit of all. Sister Consortia, who experienced the unfolding of nearly a full century during her lifetime, would approve of this rubber necking, this snooping around and getting into other people's business for the furtherance of knowledge and the good of humanity. She and her fellow sisters spent and spend their lives teaching the young by word and work, and like the human race in general, students sometimes think they have the solutions—and maybe some of them do. But if they hold keys to solving the social ills of our time, it's not because such solutions will have been dropped in their laps. It's because they will have worked with the rest of us, past and present, in finding ways to live with one another in harmony.

CHAPTER 2

AYN RAND COULD KICK KARL MARX'S ASS

OBJECTIVITY AND HISTORY

Wait…who?

Ayn Rand, author most famous for her novels *The Fountainhead* and *Atlas Shrugged*, was a pull-yourself-up-by-your-own-bootstraps and to-hell-with-everyone-else arch-capitalist of the twentieth century. Karl Marx, father of Communism and the clarion herald for worker liberation…uh… was so *not* like her.

A person's perspective also accounts for the majority of how he or she interprets the world and how history is written—how things "really" happened. Seldom, if ever, is any one account of a historical event the definitive answer that satisfies everyone. For what it's worth, I'd say Ayn Rand wins said brawl with Karl Marx because she'd kick him in the groin… pardon my gender bias.

From Caesar's *Gallic Wars*, to the various accounts of Jesus Christ, to Shakespeare's portrayals of kings, to Barbara Tuchman's *A Distant Mirror*, to our own day of political campaign advertising, human beings can only write from a limited perspective, in the midst of our struggles with memory and amnesia, in spite of our own angles and agendas and with regard to who conquered and who was conquered. All of it congeals into the stew of history.

Another simple example helps, I hope, to illustrate the issue. I can buy something "Made in America" and feel like I'm strengthening the American economy. I can also buy something "Made in Timbuktu" and pat myself on the back for helping a struggling worker in a developing country. It's all in spin, as the politicos show us *ad nauseum*.

My perceptions, my intentions say a lot about the values I hold, the message I want to communicate and the legacy I want to leave. Both purchases mentioned above, I hold, are valid. Both uphold fellow human beings and reveal our attitudes. And both attitudes hold certain responsibilities to find out how just the workers are being treated "In America" and "In Timbuktu." I'm hesitant to add, but grudgingly will give it equal time, in fairness, that it is the responsibility of both to be assured of the just treatment of the companies by their workers. History is weak in its examples of the controllers and owners of the means of production needing much assistance to attain their just rewards (short of the artisan of past centuries or the small business owner of today).

Good history needs to be as objective as possible. As stated previously, it must be as honest about biases as possible; to present material that will point future researchers, students and history nerds in the direction of further study; and, most importantly, to share with people events that have happened and are still relevant in the present.

The above Rand/Marx brawl proposes a way of seeing how capital has used any means to control labor and how labor has been lacking in ability to defend itself effectively. So this work doesn't simply try to keep a balance. I do fall on one side of the debate, no matter how objectively I try to present the material.

I don't pretend to be unbiased. The causes of civil disturbance, of which the 1886 Haymarket bombing was the most terrifying up to that time, are rooted in poverty—a poverty born of and worsened by the industrialization and mechanization wrought under the watch of capitalism in the nineteenth century. A people can be brought low and kept down for only so long. Eventually, they'll rouse themselves or be roused to action, as happened in the last quarter of the eighteenth century in the British colonies along much of the Atlantic coast of North America.

Honest history begs us not to bow down at anyone's altar, Right or Left; not to praise corporate giants who made billions of dollars while being buffered by blind justice, grotesquely bent in their favor, as they made America, as the saying goes, at the expense of millions of men, women and children slaving to earn their daily bread; and not to offer flowers and union lapel pins to the harmless memory of community leaders railroaded to their deaths on trumped up charges of murder. The eight men who were arrested, tried, convicted and executed/imprisoned for the Haymarket bombing accepted their role as standard-bearers for the anarcho-socialistic cause of worker liberation. The words of all of them and the actions of some of them tell a fuller story than has been accepted for almost a century and a half.

This saga clamors for history's stage. Part of the story (and *not* the last word by any means) is told through this book.

In Chicago, civic amnesia has been played out in past decades as major historical sites and architectural treasures fell under the wrecking ball, entombed in asphalt—progress outshining patrimony. Imperial decrees coming from the mayor's office and aldermaniac rubber stamping of those decisions up to and including our own time seem to choose municipal economic good (some ill-conceived) over a deeper, more intangible common good. The political establishment—just as hardened as concrete around the ankles of mob victims—has made honest history difficult as the memories, reputations and legal immunities of many a crony are fiddled with.

If we are to address our present problems and pressing social issues effectively, we have got to come to terms with our history, a history in

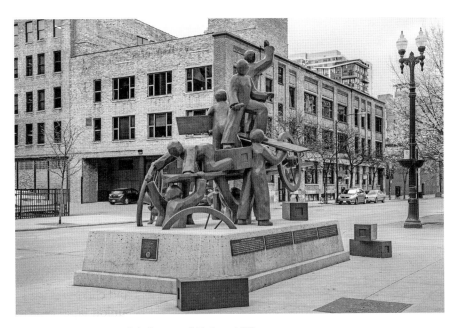

The Haymarket Memorial. *Courtesy of Nathanael Filbert.*

its entirety—the beautiful and the ugly, people behaving nobly and ignominiously, the actions that make one's heart swell with pride and those that needle us to shrink away into the shadows. History is our own story, our series of stories, a family photo album that bears everything like an Italian grandmother's arms as she's kneading dough. It's brutal, hard pounding reality that yields a beautiful, perfectly risen, steaming fresh hunk of story that tastes like paradise.

And it's in this vein that I've written *The Chicago Haymarket Affair*. With information made available through the digitization of the Haymarket trial transcripts and their easy accessibility online, now it's possible to take a more balanced look at the past events of this period in history and reassess them when necessary. I hope this work will contribute to the strengthening of our collective memory and give further context to our past for ourselves, help us address our present situations and be of benefit to future generations.

CHAPTER 3

THE WORKING CLASS SMELLS...
SO DO ROSES

THE DISCOVERERS...AND THOSE WHO KNEW
WHAT WAS ALREADY HERE

From an idea of French trader Louis Joliet in the late seventeenth century for a strategic settlement built at the junction of a big lake and a river with potential, surrounded by an onion-smelling marsh that the native population of primarily Potawatomi and Miami tribes called *checagou*, there rose one of the most prosperous cities over the next four centuries. This city would replace the settlements, grazing areas and overall open space of the people who had inhabited the region since the ice began to melt. As a play on the old saying goes, "It's all about perspective, stupid."

Who woulda thought?

Traders, trappers and others came to the area in the course of the next one hundred years after Joliet. Jean-Baptiste Point du Sable of Sainte Dominique (now Haiti) and his wife, Catherine of the Potawatomi, settled on the north side of the river (the northeast corner of Michigan Avenue). Their farmstead was central to the area's trade and integral to the growth of Fort Dearborn across the river, resulting in the incorporation of the City of Chicago in 1837 (March 4: bring a gift, pay down the debt).

During the War of 1812, the fort was evacuated, and in a battle with the Potawatomi, American troops were forced to retreat. In a perfect example of two different perspectives, this conflict of August 15, 1812, is named both "The Battle of Fort Dearborn" and "The Fort Dearborn Massacre." It was a short skirmish but resulted in the loss of the fort and the death of twenty-six soldiers, twelve militia, two women and twelve children. It was a strategic but short-lived victory for the Potawatomi.

Breeding Like...:
Chicago's Population Explosions

Over the next four decades, Chicago would become a magnet for speculators, immigrants and anyone else seeking new opportunities in this hyper-growing metropolis. The census of 1840 records 4,470 people in the city; by 1850, there were 29,963. At the start of the Civil War, there were over 112,000. By 1880, Chicago had surpassed a half million and doubled this by the time of the 1893 World's Fair.[5]

Reversing the What?!:
Audacity and Leadership in Chicago

Even though the flow of the Chicago River was not reversed until 1900, thoughts about it began as early as 1880. The city's use of the natural waterway as Mother Nature's very convenient flusher of its filth downstate enraged those who happened to live south of the urban toilet. The engineering marvel, once it was completed, opened the way for a more responsible use and preservation of the region's liquid resource. And the success of it, on the heels of the 1893 World's Fair and the literal raising of the city above its original level, was the declaration of a we-can-do-anything-we-set-our-minds-to attitude that had already manifested itself in so many ways. The 1909 redevelopment plan of the city on a grid system was the logical next step. City planners for nearly three-quarters of the nineteenth century had succeeded in bringing the natural and social environments of the area to heel by sheer acts of will. This makes a strong statement about a people's attitudes, about their expectations of outsiders and newcomers and about the drive to succeed.

Civic leadership reflected this attitude, for better and worse. As we shall see, courage, brazenness and chutzpa in the past two hundred years all had a part in making Chicago the city it is today. Skyscrapers, a century-old elevated and subterranean train system and one of the most diversified economies have rested on big shoulders for a very long time. Hercules himself would have had a time holding up this load.

Business Is Business:
Business Growth and Growing Labor Pains

The city's growth of the nineteenth century was fed by a business migration from the East Coast: the transplanted energies of Marshall Field, Cyrus and Leander McCormick, Philip Armour and others built up the sale of household goods, clothing, farm machinery and food production in Chicago. The cogs in the wheel of progress were the unending supply of laborers from the seemingly bottomless well of Irish, German and eastern and southern European immigrants; an increase of freed slaves from the former Confederacy; and white and black migrants from Chicago's neighbors to the north and across the lake.

This conglomeration of people that is Chicago's colorful labor history in the nineteenth century had its tragic side. Ethnic and racial tensions grew as owners of businesses pitted one group of workers against another in the ongoing attempt to maximize profits (for the owners) by decreasing wages (of the workers)—one of capitalism's hallowed practices. When one group of laborers began organizing and agitated for higher wages, shorter working hours or better working conditions, the owners streamlined, replacing them with a group of newcomers who would do the same job for less money and be quieter about it.

The first major labor-related conflict in the city occurred in 1855. The "Lager Beer Riot" erupted after newly elected mayor Levi Boone of the aptly named Know-Nothing Party raised the liquor licensing fees (from $50 to $300), shortened the license's term (from one year to three months)[6] and began to enforce the Sunday closing of public houses. The indirect intent of the "Prohibitory Liquor Law" was to curb the lawful assembly of the largely immigrant workers who used the pubs on their only day off for socializing and organizing.

Noncompliant tavern owners were arrested and scheduled for trial on April 21. Germans from the north side attempted an armed rescue of them at the original Cook County Courthouse on Clark and Randolph Streets but were held on the north side of the Chicago River at Clark by the swing bridge. On Boone's order, the bridge had been swung parallel with the river to split the advancing crowd (or mob, depending on one's perspective). After a short time, the bridge was returned to its position across the river and the protestors were able to cross into downtown, along with a huge mass of agitated civilians who had been trying to go about their daily business. Having gathered two hundred police officers, national guardsmen and volunteers on the river's south side, authorities ordered that the crowd of protestors be met in the streets near Courthouse Square at Randolph and Clark. In the street fighting that ensued, Peter Martens, a twenty-eight-year-old husband and father of a six-month-old, fired a shotgun at Officer George Hunt. Hunt was wounded and would later have his arm amputated. Martens was killed.[7]

As in most civil disturbances of this kind, it was unclear who fired first. Both sides have used the incident to declare the righteousness of their cause. The bloodshed of this incident was the first recorded of this scale in the city—the first time armed citizens faced off with civil authorities. The *Chicago Daily Tribune* came down strongly on the side of law and order (a phrase that would be used consistently, down to our own day) and called for the summary roundup and punishment of those involved.

At a citizens' meeting held the following Wednesday, a *Tribune* reporter described a scene whereby, after a resolution had been passed to take up a collection for injured police officers and volunteers, a man stood to speak. He was hissed at when he proclaimed that the "late riot was the legitimate growth of the lawlessness inculcated" by the recently passed ordinance. The next speaker rose to defend German immigrants, which surprised the reporter, he said, for no charge had ever been leveled against the group, though in the same article the group had been described as "invaders" and "misguided wretches" and one man an "old offender and a desperate character."[8]

Attention to issues of workers' rights increased as early as the early 1860s, in the midst of the Civil War. By 1866, organized labor in its infant stage had proposed eight-hour workday legislation in Illinois. State lawmakers passed it the following year but allowed business owners the loophole to employ laborers who would work ten-, twelve- or fourteen-hour days. The new law died within a few months and wouldn't be reintroduced with any seriousness for a generation. It would not become federal law until 1938. Over the succeeding two decades, the newborn labor movement gained momentum, and by the observance of the first Workers' Day—May 1, 1886—it was a national movement.

The Chicago Fire of 1871 devastated the city, wrought over $200 million in damage (about $3.5 billion today)[9] and left over 300 dead and 100,000 homeless (almost half the city's population). Relief came from around the world, and the Chicago Relief and Aid Society was designated by outgoing mayor Roswell Mason as the agent for the money's distribution; many local businessmen served on the board without pay during this period.[10]

By the winter of 1872, impatience grew as people felt the doling out of the relief money was too slow. Desperation from a stagnant economy, rising unemployment, ongoing poverty and the Chicago winter spurred a protest at the society's headquarters on LaSalle and Randolph Streets on December 21. Police, acting on Mayor Joseph Medill's order, herded the protesters up LaSalle and, when they had them in the tunnel that ran under the river from Water Street (now Wacker Drive) to Kinzie, began to club them into submission.

When looking back at this event, it's important to remember that people in the United States at the time, especially civil authorities, would have had fresh memories of the French Communards taking over Paris, Lyons, Saint-Étienne, Marseille and Toulouse from March 18 to May 28, 1871. In this early manifestation of what would become periodic "Red Scares" over the next century and a quarter, the American public and their elected officials protested such violence against the establishment and held firm against talk about confiscation and redistribution of private property, no matter how unbalanced the initial distribution had been.

The *Chicago Times* and *Chicago Daily Tribune* reported on December 23, 1873, a peaceful rally of about ten thousand the day before outside city hall as the city council met to discuss the relief situation. Three hundred police officers were ordered to gather; after some discussion by the mayor and his staff, it was deemed advisable to withdraw half of them.[11] A labor representative, Francis Hoffman, was allowed to address the council with the resolution from a workers' meeting held on December 21. The aldermen resolved to set up a committee to assist the Relief and Aid Society in the dispersal of funds.[12] This aura of mutual assistance and positive communication was short-lived.

In the same decade, the "Great Upheaval," the first nationwide labor strike, erupted. In mid-July 1877, West Virginian railway workers in Martinsville struck in protest of a 20 percent wage cut levied by the Baltimore and Ohio Railroad.[13] And there was no matching cut of income by ownership. The strike swept west and reached Chicago within a week. From July 24 to 28, rail workers, lumbermen, meatpackers, garment workers—men, women and children of the Second City—walked away from their jobs in sympathy with their fellow wage slaves in the East.

The Chicagoans clashed with authorities on the evening of July 25 and into the next day at Halsted Street, from 16th to 18th Streets. It was this "Battle of the Viaduct" that drew the most attention and the most blood. Here, Germans, Bohemians and Irish banded together against the superior strength of the police and Illinois National Guard. By the end of the month, the strike had been stamped out and nearly one hundred workers across the country were dead—at least fourteen in Chicago.[14]

Taking into account the Paris Commune experience of 1871, it's essential to understand the level of violence and air of rebellion that surfaced, second in this country only to the Civil War of the previous decade. Newspaper accounts testify to the fear of a revolution here and eventually swung public opinion away from the plight of the workers in favor of civil stability. As the strike had begun in the East, headlines in Chicago decried the violence while praising the situation in the Midwest as calm. With the spreading of "the fever," as it was called, newspapers intensified their fear mongering. "Red Riot," "The Insurrection," "Progress of the Riot" woke up readers in their morning routines as well as in their sense of duty to protect order.[15]

Newspaper editors tried to shame the public into abandoning any sympathy for the strikers by upholding traditional servile roles of nineteenth-century society. Women in particular were appealed to. In one report, it was estimated that 20 percent of the strikers in Chicago were female and were acting with a "wild sort of enthusiasm" and "mental aberration." Their "feminine curiosity" was endangering them and their children who accompanied them to the rallies, at which many "spoke to the officers in the most defiant manner."[16]

When push came to shove, so to speak, the public turned from the "gangs of men" moving around the city "in a high-handed manner, coercing workmen to leave their employment."[17] The establishment's most notorious victory and signal of the successful quelling of the rebellion in Chicago came near the battleground on Halsted and 12th Streets (Roosevelt Road), at a furniture workers' meeting at the Westside Turner Hall on July 26. The *Chicago Times* reported that "a mob had escaped the police" from 16th Street and tried to get into the hall where "a large communistic meeting was in progress." The police and guardsmen chased them into the hall and upstairs. The meeting's participants defended their fellow workers and tried to fight off the authorities. In a few minutes, the skirmish was over, and the wounded on both sides were attended to; two workers had been killed.[18]

In an odd exercise of equal time, a letter was printed in the *Chicago Daily Tribune* in response to a previously printed editorial. Under the pseudonym "Slug Six," the author rallied to the defense of the strikers as well as the worker-on-worker violence that was happening nationwide during the strike:

> *It is part of the general welfare…that the wages of the workers should be enough to furnish them and their families' means to buy bread and a share in the results of civilization. A dollar and a half a day won't do that, and the employed are justified in crushing those of their mates who would injure the general welfare by coming into agreement with the "bosses." The means they use may be against the law, but that counts for nothing with those who call to mind that every struggle for freedom recorded in history was a struggle against law, and that many a champion of the Good and the True has been throttled to death by that same Law. Law is blindfolded, not that she may judge impartially, but that she may not be shocked and disgusted at the deeds she does.* [19]

Table 1

Comparison of Wages 1877 and the Present

(1877 wages based on a ten-hour workday)*

Type of Work	Wages (unskilled)	Wages (skilled)	2014 (purchasing power)[20]
Sewing Girl (10–15 yrs old)	$.10/day	------------	$1.86 ($.23/hr)
Seamstress	$.30/day	$.50/day	$5.60–$9.36 ($.70/hr–$1.17/hr)
Coal Miner	$.60/day	------------	$11.20 ($1.40/hr)
R.R. Brakeman	$.80/day	$1.40/day	$14.96–$26.16 ($1.87/hr–$3.27/hr)
R.R. Mechanic	$.90/day	$1.20/day	$15.80–$22.40 ($1.98/hr–$2.80/hr)
Bricklayer	$3.00/day	$3.50/day	$56.00–$65.28 ($7.00/hr–$8.16/hr)

*When comparing with the present eight-hour shift, the 2014 amounts have been calculated to be about 20 percent less.

COMPARE WITH THE COST OF GOODS IN 1877**

Children's Socks	$.25/pair
Hosiery	$.66–$2.75/pair
Shawls and Lap Rolls	$1.00/each
Baby Carriage Afghan	$.75/each

**Cost of goods in 1877 was gleaned from advertisements in various issues of the *Chicago Times*, July 1–31, 1877.

The national railroad strike emboldened labor leaders in Chicago to fight for change through the legal means they imagined to be at their disposal. The Socialistic Labor Party garnered popular support in the city after the "Great Upheaval," as the strike had been called. Both Albert and Lucy Parsons emerged as instrumental unifiers of the disenchanted. They spoke of the importance of using the ballot to realize change. Early on, still convinced of the power of the vote, the Parsons were marked by city officials, businessmen and most newspaper owners as dangerous subversives.

In opposition to the official political stance of the Socialists, labor newspapers began to assert a sharper, more aggressive tone. The Social Democratic Printing Association on Market Street began publishing the *Chicago Socialist*. In September 1878, it condemned the practice, which recently had been made legal by the United States Congress, of allowing private citizens to buy ninety cents' worth of silver bullion and have it made into one-dollar coins.[21] Of course, this type of speculation benefited only those able to purchase large amounts of silver at this "discounted rate"—sort of a warped morphing of Roosevelt's New Deal and the twenty-first century's codification of corporate welfare.

As the decade ended, the mood in the labor landscape changed. Many in the worker movement doubted the worth of the electoral process. Leaders of the Socialistic Labor Party, after some victories at the polls late in 1877, rejected change through the electoral system by the spring of 1881, having been stung by the ballot stuffing, bribery and intimidation tactics that smothered the democratic process in Chicago.

August Spies, who would be instrumental in the drama that was to be Haymarket along with Parsons, helped organize the International Working People's Association in 1883. Out of this gathering, they published *The Pittsburgh Manifesto*, which laid out the goals of a classless society based on the cooperation among all citizens with no profit-based trade. Destruction

Lucy Parsons. *Courtesy of the Chicago History Museum.*

of propertied class rule in the capitalist structure was to be achieved by all means, "energetic, relentless, revolutionary, and international."[22]

As the call for reform and revolution intensified, the workers marshaled themselves. The "Poor People's March" on Thanksgiving Day 1884 sought to heighten awareness of the disparity between the wealthy and the poor, ownership and labor. The mansions of Chicago's rich and powerful along Prairie Avenue south of 16th Street became the focus as men, women and children walked up and down the neighborhood demanding "Work or Bread," emblazoned with the red and black banners of Socialism and Anarchism. Albert and Lucy Parsons, Lizzie Holmes and many other leaders marched at the head of nearly 1,500 people in the bold tactic of bringing the social revolution to the front steps of Chicago's social elite.[23] The modern practice of protesting outside the White House or outside a mayor's residence is an outgrowth of this earlier version.

Tensions and showmanship continued into 1885 as Chicago's major economic players celebrated, on April 28, the grand opening of the new Board of Trade building at LaSalle and Jackson (the present location of the 1930 structure). Over four hundred banqueters gathered at the Grand Pacific Hotel in the next block for a $20/plate meal. (This would be about $500/plate today.)[24] Protestors gathered at Market Square and marched to the business district's heart. A brief show of numbers, between five and six hundred, around police barriers was uneventful (save for a minor rock-throwing incident),[25] and the parade ended at the labor newspaper *Arbeiter-Zeitung* offices near Washington and 5th Avenue (now Wells Street) with speeches and interviews to newspapermen who would be called as witnesses for the state in the Haymarket trial the next year.

And this is where the tone changes. Newspaper reports followed the movement that evening of the city's anarchists as "a motley crowd of dynamiters" marching from Market Square to Adams and LaSalle. At the offices on 5th Avenue, the accounts read that Parsons and Spies "urged their hearers to arm themselves and attack monopolies." A reporter for the *Chicago Daily News*, Marshall H. Williamson, testified at the 1886 trial that Samuel Fielden (who was the last speaker at the rally when the bomb was thrown) declared, after the Board of Trade rally in 1885, that "the next time the police attempted to interfere with them they [the anarchists] would be prepared for them." Williamson asked him when that might be; Fielden said, "Perhaps in the course of a year or so." Parsons told him in the same interview that they had had enough of police interference and would use dynamite to blow up the business center of the city.[26]

Outside Chicago, in Lamont, Illinois, a quarry strike led to bloodshed on May 4—a year to the day prior to the Haymarket bombing. State militia fired on the strikers. The nonchalant tone of the report can be seen, in hindsight, as the sense of Middle America still stinging from the seemingly unpatriotic uprising of eight years previous. The *Chicago Daily News* recorded the national guardsmen's attempt "to disperse a crowd that was gathered opposite the [railroad] depot....The mob were ordered to move, but refused, and acting under instruction, fire was opened by the military."[27]

Fear increased that month as the anniversary of the fall of the Paris Commune was observed and, at the same time, funeral preparations were finalized for the great socially conscious French writer Victor Hugo, poster child of social revolution. To mark his passing, the *Chicago Daily News* focused its front-page story on fear-mongering with headlines like "More Bloodshed Feared." On the day of his burial the following week, numbers came in of those arrested (very few) who were "bearers of red flags." No instances of violence were reported as hundreds of thousands of mourners lined the streets for the nearly four-mile procession from the Arc de Triomphe to the Panthéon in the French capital.[28] The warning of the *Daily News* was only a few weeks premature.

The Streetcar Workers' Strike in early July 1885 should have served as a final warning, a thump on the city's growing shoulders that things were going poorly and deteriorating more quickly than anyone realized. Workers and passengers on the CTA's precursor protested the West Division Street Railway Company's decision to fire union leaders, cut the wages of its employees and raise fares to the public. In early June, a committee of streetcar workers had met with company officials with a list of its initial demands: the group wanted wages increased and equalized, the probationary period of new drivers and conductors shortened and the assistant superintendent of the company fired.

There was another meeting on July 23 about which the committee felt positive. However, the next day, the fifteen members of the committee were fired. On July 29, a small group of workers tried to present their demands again to Superintendent James K. Lake, of the railway company, with the added stipulation that the fifteen be reinstated. Not only were they refused a meeting with him, but they were also told to leave and watched as the executive secretary tore up their letter of demands and tossed it in the waste bin.[29]

At 4:00 a.m. on June 30, workers walked off the job and peacefully gathered at the barns on Western Avenue and Halsted, the beginning and end of a good chunk of the passenger lines, to "encourage" non-striking drivers and conductors not to take the cars on their morning runs. By mid-morning, a simmering discontent had begun to bubble. A driver at Western and Madison was pushed off his car by a crowd of around two hundred that forced the car to return to the barn. At about this time, all travel on the Milwaukee line was stopped. A Van Buren Street driver was beaten during his run, and the car was returned to the barn.[30] On Union Street, near Halsted and Madison, three thousand people blocked the tracks with paving stones, beer kegs, ash barrels and pieces of timber, along with themselves, in the largest act of defiance of the morning. Mayor Carter Harrison tried to talk to them, but they responded to his words with stones. Three cars that ventured out in the morning had all their windows broken; the horse hitched to one of them was unharnessed before the car was tipped. By noon, all cars were returned to the barns, and none would leave for the rest of the day.[31] To add fire to the already heated situation, the streetcar company accepted the flood of applicants to fill nearly one thousand positions.

Meetings were called back and forth among the mayor, the city council, the police, the company and even businessmen. President Albert Spaulding of the Chicago Base-Ball Club (later to become the Chicago White Stockings and then the Chicago Cubs) appealed to the union to run the cars for the game against Boston at the recently completed West Side Park, but American sports, in its nascent form, had no clout to sway anyone. Superintendent Lake met with police on the night of July 1 to receive assurances of the successful running of the cars in the morning. However, it was decided to suspend lines until July 3.[32]

In the meantime, on the evening of July 2, a mass rally was held at Haymarket Square. Six to seven thousand people gathered in a show of support for the strikers. Alderman (later Congressman) Frank Lawler addressed the crowd, calling for the annulment of the city's charter with the streetcar company, even though Lawler, in 1882, had voted to extend the company's charter through 1907.[33] No action was taken on this, but in an interview with reporters, the mayor confessed that the company couldn't run the cars without public sympathy because the police were incapable of ensuring their safe running on forty-five miles of street. According to his mingling with the crowd (and with rocks), it was evident to him that "nine-tenths sympathized with the strikers."[34]

In the evening newspaper accounts on Friday, July 3, the successful running of the streetcars was reported. Despite "considerable resistance" of the crowds at first, the police were able to secure traffic flow "by a liberal use of their batons." Injuries on that day were reported by the *Tribune* as eleven; the citizens ranged from a seventeen-year-old girl to a seventy-year-old man.[35]

It was decided by the mayor and the company's president, J. Russell Jones, to suspend the cars for the Fourth of July weekend due to the need of the police and fire departments' presence for supervision of the holiday festivities throughout the city.

An eerily prophetic warning was given by a police superintendent to the public in general and the anarchists specifically to "go about their business" with no congregating around corners. He went on to say, "If citizens would obey the law there would be no trouble."[36] The mayor himself, very popular at this time with the working class, defended the arrest of people for "taunting." As he said, "The policemen know that a word may cause a riot."[37] It was upon this truism that four of the Haymarket convicted would hang two years later.

By the beginning of the next week, thirty-three cars were being run on four lines. The city council and the mayor encouraged arbitration to defend the life of the company and of the workers.[38] A committee of five was set up and met in the mayor's office on the morning of the sixth, promising to report to the council that evening. Though both sides were talking, residual violence broke out. A "torpedo bomb" was detonated on the track at Van Buren and Robey (now Damen Avenue) with no injuries. About two to three hundred people gathered near there, unhitched the horse from a car and tipped it over. A little farther north, a crowd forced passengers off the car and proceeded to beat the driver and conductor in the presence of their four police officer escorts.[39]

On the evening of July 7, an uneasy settlement was reached. Both sides acknowledged misunderstandings and agreed to have the remaining differences submitted to arbitration, and the company's president promised to look into the cases of the fifteen discharged men.

Contradictory interpretation came immediately. The *Tribune* ran an editorial that proclaimed, with wagging finger, that "the alarmists who were predicting a repetition of the troubles of 1877" had been wrong.[40] On the opposite side, Lucy Parsons was quoted as condemning the agreement and saying that "the strike was a comic opera with three acts, the last one, the settlement, being a huge farce."[41] Not many people at the time could have understood the ramifications of such contrasting views that would explode the following spring.

WHAT DOES IT ALL MEAN?: HISTORICAL PERSPECTIVE AND THE HAYMARKET AFFAIR

Few heeded any of these major labor events, the volatility of the labor leaders' speeches or the violence that ensued in the decade previous. When the bomb was thrown on May 4, 1886—when labor actually struck back—people were aghast. But really they shouldn't have been surprised.

The strike of 1885 is yet another example of a people's unconquerable ignorance of their own history or anyone else's. This is something we humans seem to repeat in each generation, in every country, from the imperial Romans being caught with their togas up during the Jewish Revolt of 70 CE to the French royalty with their pantaloons down during the Revolution of 1789.

Why anyone would have been shocked that someone finally did it—that someone actually took a violent stand against forces of brutal economic oppression at a time of astronomical economic growth—is surprising. The "Gilded Age" isn't called this because of anyone's halo. Why anyone would have been taken aback at the violence and later at the uncovering of a conspiracy to usher in the social revolution at this time is the real tragedy.

Tensions ran high again on day one of the first nationwide strike for the eight-hour workday on Saturday, May 1, 1886. News reports in Chicago's daily papers marked the beginning of the new phenomenon of labor muscle with cautious observations of worker gatherings and marches. Saturday being a full workday, the stillness of the industrial areas of the city was noticeable. The quiet of Sunday, May 2, was sliced by the boisterousness of more marches, picnics and rallies. The strike's growth was noticeable, and there were a few accounts of some business owners giving in to various demands of the workers.

An increase in pay for fewer hours worked, for example, was a key component of the strikers' demands: "Ten Hours Pay for Eight Hours Worked" was the hallmark of the strike. This seemed ridiculous to economists of the day. Predictions were made of massive layoffs, the destruction of businesses and general economic chaos. Supporters of the movement claimed that with a shortened workday, everyone would have more leisure time, more money and therefore more opportunity to purchase things. It would spell economic windfall, not disaster.

SIDEBAR TIME: *It's interesting to note that the same arguments are presently coming to the fore in the "Fight for Fifteen," the debate about raising the national minimum wage to fifteen dollars an hour. It's important to note that financial adjustments were made when, in 1938, the eight-hour workday was codified by the Fair Labor Standards Act, during questionable economic times. Now it's also true that within a few years of the law's passage, we found ourselves churning at high speed toward a war economy; the point being that the economy is a malleable reality, it's adaptable and it tends to bounce back and make necessary self-corrections. I borrow that phrase from economists who tend to interpret "market behavior" with a sizeable amount of sanitized blather during periods of financial distress.*

Back to 1886: To protest another episode of violence against striking workers that occurred on May 3 at the McCormick Reaper Works near Wood Street and Blue Island Road, August Spies, who had been speaking near the south side factory, printed up a handbill—the now infamous *Revenge Circular*—to call for a public protest meeting. Spies had been present when the incident broke out. He had been asked the day before to address striking lumber shovers in a field near the reaper factory. There were a few speakers on the makeshift dais with him when the rally began in the early afternoon on that Monday.

As he spoke, the signal from the McCormick factory marking the end of the shift was heard. Some from the crowd of strikers called on their fellow workers gathered there to march on the factory and taunt the strikebreakers who had been employed at the reaper factory. Spies testified that he tried to get them to stay, but to no avail. The group split up, and those who remained with Spies were soon drawn into the rapidly deteriorating situation.

Reports vary as to what happened next, but the facts are clear that after the strikers shouted and began to throw objects at the workers coming out of the factory, the police intervened. Gunshots were heard, a larger police force appeared shortly afterward and even more gunfire was exchanged. Wisely, Spies got off the platform and ducked behind a wagon. He watched the confusion spread before him and then quickly made his way back to his printing office downtown and fired off the circular that would become a key piece of evidence against him and the others.[42]

Spies, Albert Parsons and Samuel Fielden all spoke the next night at the Haymarket meeting when the bomb was thrown. And all three, in addition to Michael Schwab, George Engel and Adolph Fischer, had been heard making comments or giving fiery speeches about the rights of workers to defend themselves from attacks of the police, militia and Pinkerton detectives. The seventh of the group of Haymarket men to be tried, Louis Lingg, made and oversaw the making of bombs in the weeks before and the day of the riot and later delivered them to Neff's Hall, where various men took several of them.

The one that was thrown, later identified from shrapnel taken from the dead and wounded, was of the exact composition as the homemade bombs later found in Lingg's room. Only one of the convicted, Oscar Neebe, was found to be outside the scope of the conspiracy charge.[43]

TABLE 2

COMPARISON OF WAGES 1886 AND THE PRESENT

(1886 wages based on a ten-hour workday)*

Type of Work	Wages (unskilled)	Wages (skilled)	2014 (purchasing power)[44]
Children	$.15/day	--------------	$3.11/day($.39/hr)
Seamstress	------------------	$.65/day	$13.52/day ($1.69/hr)
Foundry Worker	------------------	$1.25/day	$25.92/day ($3.24/hr)
Meatpacker	------------------	$1.75/day	$36.32/day ($4.54/hr)
Furniture Maker	------------------	$3.00/day	$62.32/day ($7.79/hr)

*When comparing with the present eight-hour shift, the 2014 amounts have been calculated to be about 20 percent less.

COMPARE WITH THE COST OF GOODS IN 1886**

Chicago Tribune	$.03/issue
Chicago Times	$.05/issue
Children's Gloves	$.35–$.50/pair
Adult Gloves	$.75/pair
Hats	$.45–2.85/each
Women's Shoes	$3.00/pair
Men's Shoes	$5.00/pair

Seating at McVickers' Theatre, American Opera Company Season Tickets

Gallery (Reserved), $1.00
Balcony, $2.00
Orchestra & Orchestra Circle, $2.50
Private Boxes, $15.00–20.00

**Cost of goods in 1886 was gleaned from advertisements in various issues of the *Chicago Daily Tribune*, May 1–31, 1886.

The bombing at the Haymarket meeting. *Courtesy of the Chicago History Museum.*

In the days and weeks following the May 4 bombing, a dragnet was thrown by city and state officials to catch as many potential offenders as possible in the precursor to the Red Scares of the twentieth century. The labor movement of the late nineteenth and early twentieth centuries was hamstrung after the incident. Actually, many in conventional labor unions, especially the leadership, harbored great resentment toward the Socialists and Anarchists at this time, believing them to have held the eight-hour movement hostage for their self-serving pipe dream of the workers' revolution. They really wouldn't gain back the status they had lost in the smoke of the Haymarket until the post–World War I period.

The trial neared, and after the grand jury came down with the indictments for murder, jury selection began on June 21 and was completed on July 15.[45]

A stream of witnesses for the state flowed for days as police officers, newspapermen, surgeons, citizens and former comrades of the accused testified against the eight. The defense team put up comrades, workers and labor leadership, including four of the defendants themselves, to counter the state's case. Even today, as could be expected, defenders of the Haymarket Eight have doubted the truth of much of the evidence or witness testimony that the prosecution produced; and on the other side, many have spurned the reliability of anything coming from the pro-labor, Socialist or Anarchist camps regarding the events of May 4 and beyond.

The truth is somewhere in the middle of it all. Again, because of the easy accessibility of the complete trial transcripts, something clearer can be understood. From evidence given by both sides from July 16 through August 11, it's seen that the eight accused, some more involved in a concrete plan to riot and stir a larger number to violence than the others, did advocate the abolition of the profit-based economic system through all means available—cooperative, concerted, educated and violent.[46]

It's also true, from the facts not allowed to be entered in as evidence at the trial, that the powerbrokers speaking through the mouthpiece of Chicago and national newspapers advocated the same use of violence they condemned to be brought against striking workers throughout the country over the decade preceding Haymarket;[47] and the police, state militia and hired Pinkerton detectives had used violent, subversive and abusive tactics to quell protestors, strikers and organizers, most notoriously in this era on the final day of the "Battle of the Viaduct" in 1877. No far-reaching charges or penalties were or have ever been brought against anyone from this camp.

The jury rendered its verdict of guilty on August 20. Seven of the eight men were sentenced to hang on December 3, 1886; Oscar Neebe was sentenced to fifteen years hard labor in the Joliet State Penitentiary. A stay of execution was won on November 26 when the Illinois Supreme Court agreed to hear the case on appeal. From March 4 to September 14, 1887, it deliberated and upheld the convictions and sentences. On November 2, the United States Supreme Court denied a hearing of the case, leaving the new execution date at Friday, November 11. The day before the scheduled executions, Schwab and Fielden were spared the scaffold and received life sentences after Governor Richard Oglesby read their written appeals for clemency. Lingg committed suicide in his cell that same day.

On November 11, 1887, Albert Parsons, August Spies, Adolph Fischer and George Engel were hanged in the enclosed courtyard between the courthouse and jail in the presence of witnesses who sat still and silent as the men were strangled. None of their necks broke from the hanging; after twenty-three minutes, the last of them was declared dead.[48]

Imagine what would have happened to John Hancock and the other signers of the Declaration of Independence had England defeated the colonists.

As stated previously, much of historical interpretation is in perspective: the *Pax Romana* of two thousand–ish years ago, the "Roman Peace," was only *Pax* if you happened to be *Romana*![49] And more recently, America's Manifest Destiny pushed the boundaries from shore to shore at the expense of Native American tribes; Allied forces in Europe and Asia tried to stop Germany and Japan from similar expansionism and genocide. The difference? Aside from centuries or decades in the past and a difference in genocidal method, the way history is spun—whether through textbooks, movies or political blather—makes all the difference.

Let's be honest: the real shocker is not that a bomb was thrown into a group of police at a labor meeting in 1886 but that something of this nature hadn't happened before; that somewhere in the country, after a striking worker in West Virginia had seen a co-worker bludgeoned with a night stick, or after a woman realized her daughter had been prostituting herself because of hunger, that some group of people somewhere hadn't risen up en masse, armed and red with vengeance, to confront the disparity between the wage dispensers and the wage slaves with violence.

The trial of the Haymarket Eight was a panicked attempt by conventional society to strangle the voices of protest and cripple the march of progress—and they won, for a time. The labor movement, Socialism and all voices for economic reform were cowed into submission for almost three generations. Those who did speak out on the social issues of the time—Eugene Debs, Upton Sinclair, Lucy Parsons, Mother Jones, Emma Goldman and many others—were hounded by a government, media and sheepish culture terrified of everything approaching any shade of red well into the latter half of the twentieth century.

Because of the resiliency and tenacity of workers and reformers in the United States at the turn of the century, and in spite itself, American society changed. By World War II, the eight-hour workday was law and unionization was the workplace norm. (However, some unions in organized labor did bed with organized crime for a time—and the wage slaves, once again, were the ones who got screwed.) And in spite of the combative nature of labor/owner relations today, the dream of greater cooperation among workers and the abolition of the disparity between rich and poor can still become reality.

The important thing to remember is to get to know history from as many perspectives as possible in order to approach some modicum of truth. In order that this happen, all sides must come to accept their history as honestly as possible. In a city like Chicago (and it is not the only metropolis that needs to do this), elected officials, civic leaders, police and citizens all need to look at a situation, whether past or present, and assess it with as much openness as is possible—not that is necessarily desirable but that is possible. Healing in a community can only come from an honest acceptance of personal and collective responsibility and a movement forward to change that which can be changed.

CHAPTER 4

IN THEIR FOOTSTEPS

THE SITES RELATED TO
THE HAYMARKET AFFAIR

One of my goals with this book has been to make the history of the Haymarket events come to life, in a manner of speaking…or writing. The idea for this has morphed from helping to revise an older tour book of the affair and related labor sites to doing a tour book myself (which has enjoyed a brief life in the virtual world) to the production of this book that you have in your hand. There are numerous sites related to the topic in Chicago's downtown and in the outer neighborhoods and the surrounding community. People walk past many of them daily without realizing the history underfoot or knowing little of the people who walked the same path decades or centuries before.

The following section seeks to inform fellow Chicagoans and any visitors about the reality of our past and its people, step by step, site by site, and to reconstruct the events for deeper reflection on the occurrences of the fourth of May and after.

HAYMARKET SQUARE

It's the job of the historian to strip, refresh and correct the historical record of legend, lies or lapses; some would say to smash illusions. And here's another (though it's been no secret!): the Haymarket bombing did not take place in Haymarket Square. It's just easier to say "Haymarket" Riot, "Haymarket" Bombing, "Haymarket" Affair or what have you than it is to talk about the

Haymarket Square, 1889. *Courtesy of the Chicago History Museum.*

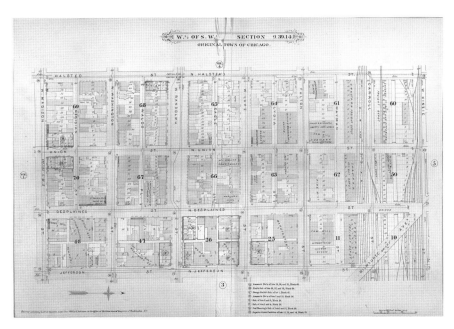

Haymarket Square, 1886. *Courtesy of the Chicago History Museum.*

"Just North of the Intersection of Randolph and Desplaines Streets" Riot, Bombing, Affair, etc. You get the picture.

In the late nineteenth century, Haymarket Square was a wide area of Randolph Street in what is today the city's West Loop neighborhood. While in the area, one has to use the imagination to block out the expressway that tore into the world of our study. Back in the day, it could accommodate a lot of pedestrian and horse-drawn vehicular traffic—sort of the Industrial Age's outdoor mall or farmers' market. It was for this reason that August Spies, the first speaker on the night of May 4, thought it best to move the rally up to Desplaines so as to not cause traffic issues and give the police an excuse to break up the meeting…and possibly some heads, as gatherings of Socialists and Anarchists tended to do back then.

There is a statue dedicated to the fallen police officers of the bombing on that night; it originally stood in the midst of the bustling street. It was unveiled on Memorial Day 1889 by the son of Officer Mathias Degan, whose death the eight men were specifically charged with. After many defacings by Anarchists, a streetcar ramming by an angry driver, two bombings by the Weather Underground and a few moves, the statue was rededicated, unveiled by a great-granddaughter of Officer Degan, on June 1, 2007, in the courtyard of Police Headquarters at 35th Street and Michigan Avenue.

THE HAYMARKET MEMORIAL

The Haymarket Memorial is just north of the northeast corner of Randolph and Desplaines Streets. After 118 years, the first government-approved marker of the event was dedicated as city and police officials, along with labor leaders, citizens, Socialists and Anarchists, gathered at the memorial statue to the Haymarket event on September 14, 2004. The sculptor, Mary Brogger, intentionally crafted the piece to be vague as to the activity (building up or tearing down) of the group of figures on the wagon.[50]

As with most things, the sculpture has not gotten universal praise due to this obscurity. But part of the value of the piece is that it's the first publicly recognized, officially "blessed" object of the events that were so divisive. The artwork actually is an expression of real history; the events have been so contested by all sides, yet the explanatory plaque and the memorial itself sum up the experience so succinctly and spread the light so broadly that one can begin to get a clearer understanding of what happened even though there is no single answer that satisfies all.

If you're in the area, stop by and take it in. Read the inscription on the east side and notice the plaques on the other three sides—particularly the west side. Watch out for Chicago drivers passing by your backside, though! There is a rally every May Day, the official International Workers' Day, according to students of history and most workers on the planet; guests from a different country and labor organization speak each year, as the plaques testify.

An interesting side note regarding the observance of the first Monday of September as Labor Day in the United States is that it officially became a national holiday in 1894 after the Pullman Porter Strike. Legislation crowning the holiday was signed by President Grover Cleveland as an attempt to slide focus away from any militant recognition of the American worker that might seep through in celebrating the first of May.

The memorial was dedicated at the site where the speakers' wagon was located on May 4. The wagon belonged to the brass and pipe fitting manufacturing facility of Richard Teller Crane and his brother, Charles. It was located on the east side of Desplaines, north of the alley.

As this book is being prepared for publication, the memorial has been temporarily relocated for its security during a construction project at the original site. For the time being, it sits at the south end of Union Park, in a narrow strip of grass at Washington Boulevard and Ogden Avenue. The monument is slated to be returned to the Randolph and Desplaines spot upon completion of the building. The plaques will be affixed to a new, larger base at that time.

At the rally, the speakers faced the crowd, looking south/southeast. When the police approached, the crowd in the street was pushed north and onto both sidewalks, east and west. This was a newly developed tactic of crowd control at the time. The tightly grouped officers would march steadily through the crowd, forming a wedge and thereby clearing the street. However, the people were pushed to the sides and eventually surrounded the police on three sides—a bit of a tactical blunder if one takes into account the volatility of the city at the time and the fed-up-ness that this group of citizens held toward the defenders of social order. Inspector John Bonfield, who headed up the group from the Desplaines Street Police Station, would be roundly criticized later for this method of street clearing.

The sidewalks in much of the city at that time were elevated about a foot above the level of the street. Of the eight officers who sustained bullet wounds or were killed by gunfire, seven received the injuries from the bullets following a downward trajectory (gunfire from a higher position than they held).[51] This forensic evidence was brought up at the trial and points logically to the fact that at least some of the citizenry were armed and contradicts past claims that no one had weapons except the police and the dead and wounded sustained the injuries from their fellow officers' own guns.

This is the part of history where we have to be honest with our heroes, on whichever side they may be. The police were acting on the legitimate fear of a civil uprising. Many were veterans of the Civil War, some were active officers during the 1877 nationwide strikes and most would have remembered afresh the streetcar strike of the previous summer. The people, for their part, were the same with a slightly different perspective: many in the crowd were foreign born and had firsthand memories or had parents who might have spoken of the civil unrest in mid-nineteenth-century Europe—the specific reason for many of them crossing the Atlantic and settling in Chicago. A large chunk of this group would have had hardened resentment toward the system and its watchmen who, in the previous decade, exercised their authority with brutal strength against protestors and strikers throughout the city. With this in mind, it's not surprising that some came to the west side armed and ready for anything.

The Alley

Let's get back to the layout of the area. The alley just south of the memorial, considering all the evidence and witness testimony, is the location where the bomb was thrown. When the bomb was thrown, it arched and came down on the west side of Desplaines near Metzner's Hardware Store, located on the northwest corner of the intersection. Two indentations were made in the street: one, an egg-shaped hole, came from the bomb hitting the wood slats in the street, and the second, a jagged and torn hole, was caused by the explosion after the bomb rolled about a foot from where it had landed. These were observed early the next morning by W.C. Metzner, the store owner, as he testified at the trial.[52] Basic geometry shows that an imaginary line drawn from one indentation to the other and then extended across the street leads to the alley (X and Y in the diagram in the following section). It's the only reasonable spot for the bomb's launching. After the bomb was thrown, it's also reasonable to assume the man slipped away in the confusion by heading east down the alley and disappearing down Randolph Street and into downtown.

From the testimony, both of the prosecution and defense, a man named Rudolph Schnaubelt (brother-in-law of one of the accused, Michael Schwab) was, and still is, believed to be the bomb thrower. He was arrested early in the investigation but was released and left the city before the link between him and the bomb was forged. His whereabouts afterward have never been definitively shown.

Harry Gilmer testified that he identified Schnaubelt from a picture of him Gilmer was shown before leaving the Central Police Station after Schnaubelt had already been released.[53] Gilmer also stated that he saw Spies get down from the speakers' wagon and walk to the alley. When the police approached, Gilmer swore that he saw Spies light the fuse and Schnaubelt throw the bomb. The defense spent a lot of time and energy trying to discredit Gilmer's reliability while the prosecution attempted to bolster it. In the end, for both the defendants and the prosecution, it was irrelevant because the conspiracy charge brought the canvas of culpability over Spies anyway due to his speeches and, as the prosecution showed, the articles published in the Anarchist newspapers.

It was assumed that finding witnesses who could place the bomb thrower as far away from the speakers' wagon as possible would be to the defendants' advantage. With Metzner's testimony, it became irrelevant as well. In addition, as Judge Gary explained and as the prosecution successfully proved, for the men to be found guilty on a charge of conspiracy to riot and commit murder, the identity of the one who threw the bomb need not be discovered.[54]

Regardless of who the bomb thrower was, the fact that a massive amount of gunfire began at just about the same time as the explosion points further to the probability that what happened on the night of May 4 was either a planned attack/riot/uprising or a situation in which a group of people anticipated interference from the police, as had happened often in the city's

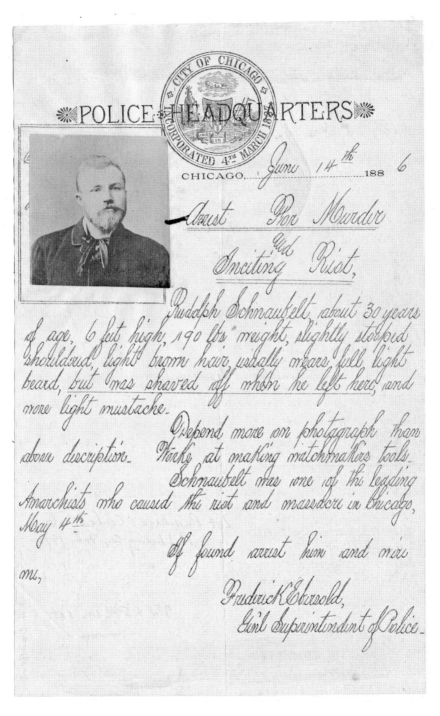

POLICE HEADQUARTERS

CITY OF CHICAGO · INCORPORATED 4TH MARCH 1837

CHICAGO, June 14th 188 6

Arrest For Murder
and Inciting Riot,

Rudolph Schnaubelt about 30 years of age, 6 feet high, 190 lbs weight, slightly stooped shouldered, light brown hair, usually wears full light beard, but was shaved off when he left here, and wore light mustache.

Depend more on photograph than above description. Works at making matchmakers tools.

Schnaubelt was one of the leading Anarchists who caused the riot and massacre in Chicago, May 4th

If found arrest him and wire me,

Fredrick Ebersold,
Gen'l Superintendent of Police.

Rudolph Schnaubelt. *Courtesy of the Chicago History Museum.*

past and workers' memories. No one's memories—based on the testimony of the police, citizens, reporters or accused—agreed on whether the explosion occurred first or the gunfire began it all. Again, proving the sequence of the two events was not essential to the prosecution's case.

THE DESPLAINES STREET POLICE STATION AND THE MARCH

The Desplaines Street Police Station doesn't exist anymore. One must imagine the sight of the police marching up Desplaines, about half a block south of Randolph, to break up the meeting around 10:15 p.m. that night. It had been a warm day, but by the time the police left the station, the weather had begun to turn. Minutes before, Parsons had interrupted Samuel Fielden, the final speaker, to suggest they move the meeting into Zeph's Hall at the corner on Lake Street. Fielden said he would wrap up his address and all could disperse afterward. Albert and Lucy Parsons and a few others left the gathering and headed toward Zeph's.

The movement of the police would have been slightly lit up by the numerous electric light bulbs at the entrance of the Lyceum Theatre about a block south of the station, on the opposite side of the street. Seven companies of officers, almost 180 men, moved up Desplaines. The captains, front company lieutenants and some officers stopped just north of the alley alongside the wagon. The command was given for the crowd of about 200 to disperse. Fielden defended the passivity of the meeting and got down. The bomb was thrown at this time, and gunfire followed almost immediately after the explosion.

From this point, the area was a battleground. Those inside the hall tried to escape the building but found the back door locked. A side door was opened, and most fled north on Desplaines or east on Lake. Those who had heard Fielden up to the time of the officers' approach fought and then fled mainly west, north and east. The police dragged each other south, back toward the station, which served as jail, hospital and morgue.

The five physician-surgeons and the county physician who testified at the trial gave graphic detail as to the bullet and shrapnel wounds of the officers they treated both at Desplaines Station and at Cook County Hospital in the ensuing days and weeks. Their testimony has always been present in the trial transcripts, but again, it's part of a large chunk of the trial that has been omitted by most scholars until the Chicago History Museum digitized them and made them readily available at the tip of our fingers (literally, on any electronic device).[55]

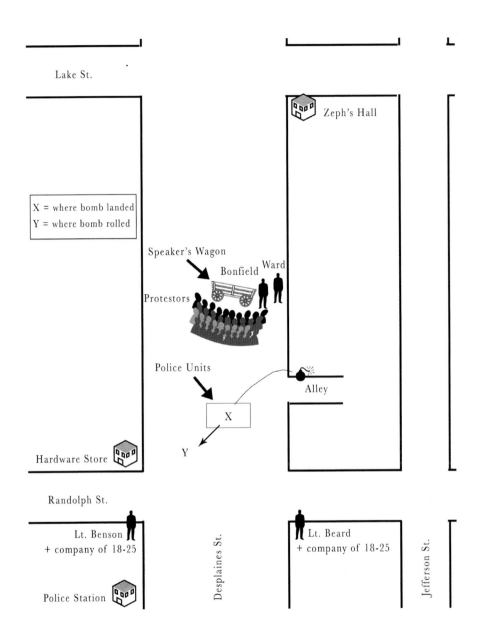

Their testimony and the description of the wounds contradict the traditional assumption that the officers' casualties were sustained at one another's hands, unwittingly firing at their comrades in arms in the panic of combat, and that the civilian dead and wounded were caused by the police as well.

It's a bit of a stretch to hold both positions—that, on the one hand, the police were in a panicked flight after the bomb went off and shot one another in the confusion and that, on the other hand, in the midst of this chaos they had the wherewithal to fire at the crowd. One of these two things has to give way to fact: either the police panicked and shot at their own, then limped back to the station to lick their wounds and care for the dead, which leaves unexplained the number of civilian casualties and the street sweep that was carried out until past midnight; or the police held their ground and fired *back* into the crowd that had begun to fire at them. As stated before, it's unimaginable that with the level of frustration and anger at the established order in 1886 Chicago and the memories of past abuse fresh in their minds, a group of people—several of them radical Anarchists—would have come unarmed to a rally at a tense period of the city's life. It's possible, one could suppose, but not likely.

Those who remained on the street chased down anyone without a uniform. By midnight, most of the area was quiet. Citizens fled and didn't return. Casualties from the crowd have never been nor probably ever will be determined due to fear and secrecy. Treatment of the wounded would have been sought at neighborhood apothecaries and at home out of fear of police presence and later official inquiries at hospitals for gunshot or shrapnel wounds treated.[56]

This is an important element in the Metzner testimony about his pre-dawn observations. While there was no Crime Scenes Investigation section of the police department, no "yellow tape," much of the evidence remained unscavenged by souvenir hunters in those early hours after the bombing. What he saw was as pristine a situation as it could have been, and his testimony ended much of the lengthy debate as to the whereabouts of the bomb thrower.

ZEPH'S HALL

Zeph's Hall is one of the few buildings directly connected with the Haymarket Affair still standing. This hall was a major meeting place for several trade unions at the time. As stated above, the Parsonses, Lizzie Holmes and a friend named Thomas Brown went there for a short time before the violence erupted down the street. After the explosion and

Zeph's Hall. *Courtesy of Nathanael Filbert.*

gunfire, they left the building and headed north on Desplaines to Kinzie. It was there, Brown testified under cross-examination, that he gave Albert Parsons five dollars to help him leave the city as Parsons had been counseled by Lucy to do.[57] Parsons would meet up with William Holmes, Lizzie's husband, in Geneva, Illinois, and not return to Chicago until the opening of the trial in July.

As stated before, this was one of the greatest blunders of the defense. Not only was it in their clients' best interest to have at least two separate trials, but once it was decided to have the seven men (prior to Parsons's return) tried at the same time, Parsons could have returned a day later and been granted a separate trial automatically.

At the trial, which of the defendants were inside Zeph's, who saw whom there and when they saw them all became major points of attack for the prosecution and repelling for the defense. There was security in claiming that person X was inside the hall when the bomb was thrown (for obvious reasons), but it gave little protection under the barrage of testimony that seemed to indicate the bombing was the result of a conspiracy—and from this there was little refuge.

GRIEF'S HALL: WHISPERS OF CONSPIRACY

Grief's Hall, originally located on the northwest corner of Lake and Clinton Streets, was another one of Chicago's numerous union halls where workers used to socialize, eat/drink, organize—and, in the case of some, conspire to meet the brutality of the police with an equalizing force. Never before this period had more hope been given to a rebellious element than with Alfred Nobel's invention of the mid-nineteenth century. Dynamite revolutionized the mining and railroad industries in clearing rock and literally moving mountains. It also gave never-before-imagined hope to a growing revolutionary movement across Europe, especially in a newly united German Empire and Tsarist Russia, as well as post–Civil War America. The power of this substance, the ease of its use and the low cost of its manufacture allowed a unique opportunity of explosive outlet to the growing restlessness of the western world's working classes.

It was inside Grief's, in the basement, that a meeting was held on May 3, just hours after the violence at the McCormick Reaper Works had occurred. Several witnesses for the state gave testimony ("squealed" or "did their patriotic duty," again depending on one's perspective) of a "Monday Night Conspiracy Meeting" that took place the night before the bombing. Now, there was no uprising of armed workers throughout the city after the McCormick incident. The prosecution admitted this in its arguments about conspiracy. It never had to prove that there was a set plan to revolt on the night of May 4 or any other specific day. The only element necessary for the state's attorney to show in order for the accused to be found guilty was the presence of an agreement to riot at any time and that the accused—through their words and, on occasion, some of their actions—egged on, in a sense, the unleashing of violence.[58]

It had been decided to use a secret code word (*ruhe*, German for rest or sleep) printed in the German workers' paper *Arbeiter-Zeitung*, signaling the armed groups that the time had come to gather and prepare to fight. This meeting at Grief's provided the prosecution with a large swath of material out of which the conspiracy charge was woven. The defense, however, argued that Spies, once he found out what *ruhe* signaled, ordered Fischer to inform the groups to disregard it.

Wehrer and Klein Printers: Get That in Writing

The Wehrer and Klein Print Shop was located on Lake Street, east of the river at Market Street (Wacker Drive). Another piece of damning evidence came in the form of a circular, or handbill, that was distributed in the morning of the fourth. One handbill has already been referred to, the *Revenge Circular*, which Spies wrote and printed when he returned to the *Arbeiter-Zeitung* offices shortly after the McCormick violence. Adolph Fischer, on Tuesday morning, May 4, took the master copy of a second circular announcing the Haymarket rally from the *Arbeiter-Zeitung* offices to the print shop on Lake. August Heun, a printer at the shop, testified to the key wording in German and English that the prosecution clung to for its case: "Workingmen Arm Yourselves and Appear in Full Force." Later on, as the defense showed, by the protests of Spies, a change was ordered and the "Arm Yourselves" line was eliminated. Heun testified that the reworded circular was brought in for printing about an hour after the original had been.[59]

Many of these originally phrased copies were confiscated by the police and used against the defendants. It's important to remember that state and

Left: The *Revenge Circular. Courtesy of the Chicago History Museum.*

Right: The May 4 handbills. *Courtesy of the Chicago History Museum.*

federal law at that time interpreted the Fourth Amendment (protection against unlawful searches and seizures) broadly enough to protect the right of the state to defend civil order over individual liberty.[60]

An interesting side note in the area where the print shop was located is on Wacker Drive about half a block south of Lake. At the corner building, 191 North Wacker, there is a plaque surrounded by some landscaping. It marks the sites of the Sauganash Hotel (1830–51), which housed the city's first theater and, later, the Wigwam, the building where the Republican Convention nominated Abraham Lincoln for the 1860 presidential election. (He won, btw.)

MARKET SQUARE AND THE MOUSE TRAP

As in much of the city, one has to use the imagination to envision the streetscape of 1886 Chicago. At the time of our study, the level of the city was pretty much the level of the river. In the area of what was then Market Square (the present-day Lyric Opera), the land was clear and served as another of the city's gathering/selling/milling about kind of places. Remember that Upper and Lower Wacker hadn't been invented yet, although Daniel Burnham would begin to dream, not too far from this time, of such a thing. Market Street bounded the square on the east side, and the river formed its western limit.

As Haymarket Square was not, Market Square was a perfect location for gatherings of large groups. It wasn't so cramped and clogged with traffic. Albert Parsons addressed a crowd of strikers and sympathizers during the 1877 Railroad Strike; Socialist leaders used the space again to launch the 1885 rally and protest march against the grand opening of the newly built Board of Trade building; and the Poor People's Marches on Thanksgiving Day in 1884 and 1885 began here. On the evening of May 3, at the Grief's Hall basement meeting, it was first proposed as the site for the protest rally but was soon rejected as being "a mouse trap." It was felt that in the likely event of the police advancing against the strikers to disperse them, there would be no path of retreat for the people.[61] Again, the prosecution used the testimony of some of the companions of the accused to strengthen its case of conspiracy: the fact that this site was rejected as a place to hold the rally showed clearly that the organizers anticipated violence and had planned for it and made preparations for strategic fight and flight.

"NEWSPAPER ROW"

There is a strip of Washington Street east of the river that hosted several daily newspapers. It's the site of the offices of the *Chicago Times*. The building stood on the north side of the street west of Wells Street (formerly known as 5th Avenue). The *Times* was one of the city's many daily papers. As with the *Tribune* and most other papers, the *Times*, owned by some of Chicago's most powerful men, wrote vehemently anti-labor editorials for years before the bombing. It was among the contributors to the local and national tone that hanged the accused long before the ropes were around any of their necks.[62]

Another of the city's papers, though with a different focus and audience, was the labor paper, the *Staats-Zeitung*, located at the northeast corner of Washington and Wells Streets. Established in 1848, this German-language newspaper supported the rights of workers, though not as militantly as one of its more notorious sister papers, the *Arbeiter-Zeitung*. The *Staats-Zeitung*, though less vehemently anti-capitalistic, staunchly defended the Haymarket Eight during the trial, the appeal and throughout the movement to win them clemency before the execution.

Down Wells Street, just south of Washington about half a block, on the east side of the street, stood the three-story office building of the Socialistic Publishing Company and the workrooms of the *Arbeiter-Zeitung*, *Die Fackel* and the *Alarm*. These German and English labor newspapers were published on the second and third floors of the original building. From here, Adolph Fischer took the circular announcing the rally to the Wehrer and Klein print shop at Lake and Market. The police raided this building and searched the offices on May 5, seizing papers, flags, dynamite, fuses and caps (without warrants but with probable cause and under martial law declared that morning, soooo...). Authorities arrested everyone connected with the company and its affiliate papers either in their homes or in the building over the course of the following few days and released most over the ensuing weeks. Numerous articles from the *Arbeiter-Zeitung* and the *Alarm* were entered as evidence against the accused.[63]

CENTRAL POLICE HEADQUARTERS

The site of the Central Police Headquarters is the whole block encompassed by Washington, Randolph, LaSalle and Clark Streets, which is now the Cook County Building and City Hall. Though not the same building, this is the spot where Spies, Fischer, Fielden, Schwab and Neebe were taken, held and questioned. (Engel and Lingg were arrested in mid-May and brought to the Chicago Avenue Station.) In their basement cells, the prisoners were interviewed by members of the press; some of these newspapermen were later called in as witnesses for the state during the trial. The protection of individuals arrested and questioned would not be solidified until the 1966 Supreme Court decision in *Miranda v. Arizona*, which guarantees the rights to silence and legal counsel. To the detriment of those arrested at this time, a good amount of seized evidence (again, unwarranted) was taken from the defendants' homes and offices, kept here and later brought into the courtroom during the trial.

When looking back at an event, while it's very easy to judge it or a people in the past through the lenses of our present practices and insights, we must come to its study with more objectivity and understanding. Again, much of the practice of law at the time gave the weight of protection to civil order and the propertied class. Much evidence and testimony was allowed into the trial that today wouldn't be permitted. Jurisprudence changes with societal need; what is protected and who is held responsible depends on a particular people at a particular period of their history.

The American Civil War had been fought only a generation earlier. National strife due to labor issues had exploded less than a decade before, and an enormous population of immigrants swept across the Atlantic Ocean with a lot of energy and angst—some with an international sense of worker liberation. Threats to social order seemed to be constant, and therefore, the guardians of that order felt they had to be vigilant, a lot of times to the detriment of individual liberty. And, historically, whenever public safety comes up against personal freedom, it's the individual person whose rights are usually suppressed.

As another brief sidebar, I give you some examples: The Alien and Sedition Act of 1798, which greased the government's ability to deport foreign-born troublesome people and restricted an immigrant's ability to vote. Most of the act would remain in effect through the nineteenth century. Both the Espionage Act of 1917 and the Sedition Act of 1918 crippled the right to protest the United States' entering into and profiting from the First World War. The Patriot Act of 2001 (and still in effect, with slight emendations) gives the government an increase in power to fight international terrorism. Lest one think it hypocritical, these examples are given only to show the choice a particular group of people is more likely to make at a particular period of history. All nations and peoples act in similar fashion; I only highlight one.

Back to the sites.

THE LASALLE STREET TUNNEL

The site of the LaSalle Street Tunnel is located on the south section of LaSalle Street at Kinzie. Though not directly connected with the Haymarket Affair, it's an interesting piece of the downtown story. Standing on the east side of LaSalle on Kinzie, one can look to the left and see what remains in small form of the tunnel that was completed early in

1871 as a pedestrian thoroughfare underneath the river. Its value was realized almost immediately when, during the fire that autumn, it became a major escape route for fleeing refugees. City officials used the tunnel more ignominiously during the winter of 1872–73 to quell the "Bread Riot," the march on the city's Relief and Aid Society when protestors were driven away from the headquarters at LaSalle and Randolph and into the tunnel. Presently, there is an entrance to a parking garage that utilizes the subterranean space. It's a remarkable example of possibly the only historical site in the world *preserved* by a parking garage!

Nearby, just west of the intersection on Kinzie and across LaSalle west of the river at Desplaines Street was the spot where Albert Parsons was counseled on the night of the fourth by his wife, Lucy, and their comrades Lizzie Holmes and Thomas Brown to flee the city for a while. He would not return until the opening day of the trial.[64]

THE COOK COUNTY COURTHOUSE, JAILHOUSE AND EXECUTION COURTYARD

The site of the trial, incarceration of the accused during the proceedings and hangings of four of them occurred here at the northwest corner of Dearborn and Hubbard Streets. The structure that stands today is the third courthouse building on this site. It was built in 1892, using some of the stone from the second structure (1874) in which the Haymarket trial occurred. The original courthouse on this site burned in the 1871 fire. In the vestibule of the present building, there is a photo gallery of some of the famous trials that took place in the second and third courthouses; the west wall, in particular, has pictures related to the Haymarket Affair. The jail was behind the courthouse with an enclosed courtyard connected to it. The four men were hanged in the courtyard.

As far as the trial itself went, as stated previously, it was legal for the time. The allowance of evidence obtained without warrant was permitted because of probable cause. Testimony given in interviews and without legal counsel was used against the accused because the practice wouldn't be challenged successfully for eight decades. It is important to balance the historical record here about the sitting judge, Joseph E. Gary's behavior, which has received such attention in the past. It's been assumed that he was not attentive to the proceedings, but again, a thorough reading of the transcripts shows him in control and sensitive to explanation of the law and his reasons for sustaining or overruling objections from both the defense and prosecution.

According to the transcripts, the defense had originally petitioned the court for and was granted a new judge (Gary) because, as it alleged, the originally assigned judge, John G. Rogers, was prejudiced against its side.[65] Judge Gary's behavior, upon a thoughtful reading of the transcripts, shows that he displayed a clearer understanding of Illinois and federal law in relation to the case than has been previously granted him. On several occasions, he stopped the proceedings to explain to the defense the conspiracy charge and why it was not necessary to identify the bomb thrower for the eight men to be convicted. In a story on the final day of jury selection, a reporter summarized Gary's instruction: "That the existence of a conspiracy to annihilate the police force and destroy property rendered the defendants, who were the instigators in it, liable for an act looking to such annihilation, even if committed without their specific sanction at that particular time and place."[66]

Gary himself would further explain later on during the trial: "If that one offense [conspiracy to revolt and commit murder] was incident to a larger plan, then the investigation of that one offense lets in everything."[67]

Contemporary newspaper reports of the day of the execution, "Black Friday," November 11, 1887, are quite detailed and communicate the tension in the city that morning. The entire block of Hubbard, Dearborn, Clark and Illinois Streets was cordoned off, with sentries posted at intervals in the roped-off area, as well as some stationed on the rooftops in the surrounding streets. Anyone who was allowed to witness the execution (reporters, police, city officials, clergy and attorneys) was given a pass that got them behind the rope and then to the courtyard gate, through the gate and into the courtyard and to a chair.

The family members of the convicted were allowed to visit with the condemned the morning of the execution—all except Lucy Parsons and her and Albert's two children. She was told at a police station the day before to come in the morning. When she approached the rope, she was told that the visit was not possible. A reporter wrote of her anger and anguish at not having been allowed Albert's, her or the children's farewell.

The report of the hanging is grisly and tragic. For whatever reason (speculated by both sides of the issue), the nooses were tied in such a fashion that none of the necks of the men broke. They were strangled by the ropes and died quite slowly. The enclosed courtyard was silent, even after the last of them was declared dead.

Some words here are necessary to correct a prevalent but little understood historical fact. After the conviction from the initial trial, the defense went about preparing the appeal as was its duty to its clients. It spent the fall of 1886 and the spring of 1887 doing just that. The appeal documents were basically a summary of the trial transcripts—mainly the points where it filed exceptions during the first trial. Now, a thorough reading of the transcripts shows many points (far out of the scope of this brief study) where the defense objected to a particular juror chosen (as has already been covered and referenced), the prosecution's questions or method of questioning, the evidence allowed in or the judge's rulings on particular points.

When there came time for one of the eight men's comrades, Dyer Lum, to publicize the trial—partly as a fundraising effort to help with the appeal costs—he wrote *A Concise History of the Great Trial of Chicago Anarchists in 1886*. His source for this work was the defense's summary of the trial it had prepared for the appeal.

Lum's work was used as the main source for historians until 2011. Consequently, any chronicling of the events has been skewed more than should be expected. This is simply what has developed. Historians built upon what they found. There wasn't a worldwide conspiracy to fool the world into sympathizing with the poor wretches' fates any more than the four gospel writers set about to fool millennia of people into following a Jewish carpenter.

The original work on any subject is what it is. What others have done with a particular work is what has been. As we progress in historical or literary knowledge and experience and hone the tools we use, we have a responsibility to adjust the record. There is no proclamation to tear down statues or rip up sacred books, to abandon causes or ditch faith, but only to look at those things we cherish—and our common stories should be among those treasures—and see them afresh. And this is the time in which to reevaluate the Haymarket story.

Timothy Messer-Kruse's work on the trial shines a scholarly spotlight on this issue as he shows various points from Lum's book in comparison to the appeal summary and then to the trial transcript. It's similar to the natural inaccuracies and oversights of translations—the further one gets away from the original copy of a document in its original language, the fuzzier the meaning becomes.[68] (I give you the numerous examples of biblical translations, some of which are more accurate than others depending on their faithfulness to the Hebrew, Aramaic or Greek originals.)

So what has happened over the past 130 years is a history-recording oddity—an incident whereby someone who didn't "come out on top" has written the history. The saying that "History is written by the winners" has its exception in the Haymarket Affair. And how appropriate it has been that a people's story of a moment in their history when forces could have brought down the capitalist structure was told by the people themselves. Well, since it's no one people's story to tell—it belongs to the collective "us"—it becomes the duty of objectivity to tell the fuller story.

The Revere House Hotel

The jurors were sequestered in the Revere House Hotel originally located on the southeast corner of Hubbard and Clark Streets. The 1874 hotel, built after the fire, remained in operation until 1949 after a fire in the building the year before damaged most of it. In another historical side note, Eugene Debs, the nation's greatest Socialist leader, roomed at the Revere in 1894 while leading the Pullman Porter Strike. For this he would serve six months in federal prison (for the strike, not for staying at the hotel). His conviction and imprisonment came about as the result of Grover Cleveland's ending the strike by attaching mail cars to the passenger train and thereby putting the system under federal jurisdiction. Debs was arrested for defying the injunction and was imprisoned. He would go on, over the next two decades, to run for president of the United States in every election from 1900 through 1920, with the exception of 1916. He is the only U.S. presidential candidate to run while in prison; he had been arrested in 1918 for protesting American involvement in the First World War, which was illegal at the time. He was released in 1921.

The facts related to juror selection for the Haymarket trial have been muddled over the past century due to the simple fact that the procedure of choosing them, until recently, hasn't been studied as thoroughly as one would expect. Traditionally, it's been assumed that the jury was stacked against the eight accused, that the twelve who would sit in judgment were chosen specifically for their pro-capitalist beliefs and that they were all part of the elite class. But a glance at the list of the men who were eventually chosen out of the 982 examined and the occupations they held shows mainly a group of middle management types, salesmen and shopkeepers.[69]

The entire section related to choosing jurors runs for over 2,200 transcript pages and reveals the defense's liberal use of its right to challenge a juror, engaging in discussion about a man's objectivity where Socialism and Anarchism were key elements of the charges. Judge Gary is clear in his discussions with William Black of the defense about legal presumption of innocence, knowledge of the event at hand and the ability of particular jurors to be impartial in judging the presented evidence and testimony during the trial.[70]

The judicial system had the tricky task of balancing the individual liberty of each of the accused in addition to upholding the law of a society that felt itself under attack from forces bent on its destruction. A generation after bloody civil war, less than a decade after a violent nationwide strike that brought industry to a standstill in 1877 and half a decade after the assassination of a second American president alongside news from Europe of similar attacks of crowned heads, the guardians of social order were a tad edgy, shall we say.

But the system doesn't have a good record of honestly assessing a situation in a given time; over and over again, those in power have reacted to keep themselves enthroned rather than acting for the good of the social order in the long run. Thomas Jefferson, in crafting the Declaration of Independence, left open the possibility that the government he was proposing, and the other signatories would approve, might need to be overhauled—there might come a time when the particular setup ran out of time. Those who hold power rarely can see that possibility manifesting itself, so they react to preserve the power structure as it stands.

It's good to serve warning here of the danger of anachronism: we cannot judge too harshly the procedures of our forbearers when they differ from our present practices. It's very simple to disparage these practices. It is true that the Haymarket trial would have probably had a different outcome today than it did in 1886, but in some ways it might not have been different—bombs were still made, one of the devices was used against the police. For whatever reasons, a second American Revolution might have been sparked. But it didn't play out this way. The twelve jurors were able to swear that they could judge the evidence as it was presented, even though both the defense and prosecution tried to make the case a judgment of Socialism and Anarchism.

We view juror objectivity differently; but before we get too smug about our enlightened ways, it's important to admit that potential jurors today can be even less objective than one hundred plus years ago. Before we judge too harshly a process flawed because of journalistic hyperbole (to sell more newspapers), we must be honest about our own foibles resulting from the quick and often more exaggerated information that is so easily accessible (bits of it are even accurate!) about high-profile cases. All in all, with any trial, the system is set up to give as just a hearing as possible, striving to protect the rights of the individual and society, to be fair to both the accused and the community.

The Seliger House (Bomb-Making Central)

The home that was the site of Louis Lingg's bomb-making is no longer standing. The address would be 1544 North Sedgwick, near the southwest corner of Sedgwick and North Avenue, steps away from the Sedgwick Brown Line station. Lingg rented a room in the home of William and Bertha Seliger. From the couple's testimony, the bombs were made in various places in the house, including Lingg's room and the kitchen. William Seliger and several other men took part in the bomb construction and assembly under Lingg's direction during the morning and afternoon of May 4. Around 8:30 p.m., Lingg and Seliger carried thirty to fifty bombs in a trunk down North Avenue to Neff's Hall on Clybourn Avenue, another of the city's labor meeting places. Before they got to the hall, they would have had to pass the police station at Larrabee Street and North Avenue, which will be covered below. According to Seliger's testimony, Lingg talked of his desire to throw bombs into the station as they walked by. They didn't and so continued south on Clybourn.

In the days following the riot, police searched the house and found more bomb-making implements, lead pipes, fuses, blasting caps and powder, as well as finished bombs. Again, the metallurgic composition of the bombs found in the house was identical to the composition of the metal shrapnel removed from the dead and wounded officers. The types used all over the world at the time of the birth of this new weapon were mainly two: a simple pipe bomb, using any length of gas or other pipe, and a "czar bomb," in recognition of the Russian use of the round version in the assassination of Czar Alexander II in 1881.

After dropping off the bombs, Lingg and Seliger went back north on Larrabee, across North Avenue about six blocks, to the intersection of Larrabee, Webster and Lincoln. The Webster Street police station was around here. Lingg and Seliger stopped at a saloon near the station for a beer. Sadly, as happens, nothing remains of either the police station or saloon. They kept a few bombs in their coats. Their comings and goings that night were laid out by William Seliger at the trial.[71]

Again, this is an area of the history that has been hotly contested through the insistence that the prosecution bribed witnesses and promised them immunity from prosecution in exchange for their damning testimony. With no video surveillance from this time available to us, we have limited sources from which to put together the events as close to how they happened. One of the main pieces to reconstructing this mystery is witness testimony. I don't think we can discount some of the words of a particular group solely because of what was at stake for them. If that were the case, nary a mobster, drug lord or politician would be in prison. There has to be some balance between an individual's testimony, the consistency of a particular narrative and that person's motivation in speaking. It would be just as true for the defendants themselves. Their words cannot be discounted simply because they were the accused and were trying to save themselves.

The Larrabee Street Police Station

The site of the Larrabee Police Station is on the northwest corner of Larrabee and North Avenue. Again, following Seliger's testimony of that night, he stated that after having the beer, he and Lingg returned to this intersection. It would have been around 10:40 p.m., as they witnessed the patrol wagon full of officers that had been ordered to leave the station and head south, Lingg assumed, to the Haymarket. When the patrol wagon passed, they were standing on the south side of North Avenue, and Lingg intended to throw a bomb at the wagon. He ordered Seliger to light a match for him to ignite one of the bombs in his coat. Seliger lost his nerve and stalled, stepping into an enclosed area, pretending to be unable to light his cigar. The wagon passed without incident.

Infuriated, Lingg returned to the Seliger house with him; Lingg showed Seliger a copy of the *Arbeiter-Zeitung* with the *ruhe* signal word, explaining its meaning to be ready to act because the time to revolt had come. After seeing the patrol wagon leave the station, Lingg was convinced that something had happened on the west side. They went back to Neff's Hall, where they found an agitated gathering of men who informed them about the bombing. One of them went so far as to blame Lingg for the whole thing. Lingg and Seliger left the hall around midnight and walked back to Sedgwick with some of the bombs. They hid them under the sidewalk on Siegel Street, between Sedgwick and Hurlbert.

Another witness for the state, Gustav Lehman, would accompany Officer Michael Hoffman to a prairie in the area around the corner of Clyde and Clybourn (Ogden's Grove) where Lehman had hidden bombs and bomb parts in the middle of the night after the riot.

Over the course of the next few weeks, citizens and police found numerous pipe bombs, loaded and unloaded, along with canisters, coils of fuses and boxes of detonating caps, in the areas of what is today Wicker Park, Old Town and River North.[72] Much of this was displayed in the courtroom, with much consternation from some of the public, as could be imagined. It didn't help the cause of the defendants that such devices and parts of weapons were found in the offices of the Socialistic Publishing Company. Spies had kept pipe bombs in his desk and showed them to visiting reporters for publicity and bravado. He also had admitted to taking some to the lake and detonating them as experiments to see their effects. For him and the others, the effects were more explosive than simply from blasting caps.

NEFF'S HALL

Another one of the city's German labor meeting places, Neff's Hall, located at present-day 1265 North Clybourn Avenue, still stands. Lingg and Seliger arrived here shortly after 8:30 p.m. on the evening of the bombing. They brought in the trunk and set it down in a passageway near the entrance. Three or four men were seen reaching into the trunk and taking out various pipe and round bombs. One of the men, more than likely, was Rudolph Schnaubelt, the almost-100-percent-believed bomb thrower. Remember, the composition of the bomb that was thrown a short time later at the Haymarket rally matched the composition of the bombs found in Lingg's room, as well as the various weapons recovered throughout the city in the subsequent weeks. It was Seliger's testimony about these events that was damning for Lingg and, by association in the conspiracy theory, for six of the other seven as well.

It's a sobering fact to admit that with all the evidence against Lingg himself as far as his direct culpability in making the actual device that was used in the incident is concerned, the defense counsel didn't seek a separate trial for him alone—if for no other reason than to distance its other seven clients from the fallout of his actions. Lingg never denied his actions or his intentions. In fact, at the end of the trial when all the convicted were given a chance to make statements, he used his closing words to throw down:

> *I tell you frankly and openly, that I am for force. I have already told Captain* [Michael] *Schaack, "If they use cannon against us, we shall use dynamite against them." I repeat that I am the enemy of the "order" of today, and I repeat that, with all my powers, so long as breath remains in me, I shall combat it. I declare again, frankly and openly, that I am in favor of using force…we shall dynamite you. You laugh! Perhaps you think,* "You'll [emphasis in transcript] *throw no more bombs;" but let me assure you that I die happy on the gallows, so confident am I that the hundreds and thousands to whom I have spoken will remember my words; and when you shall have hanged us, then, mark my words,* they will do the bomb throwing! [emphasis in transcript] *In this I hope do I say to you:* "I despise you. I despise your order; your laws; your force-propped authority." [emphasis in transcript] *HANG ME FOR IT!*[73]

Neff's Hall. *Courtesy of Nathanael Filbert.*

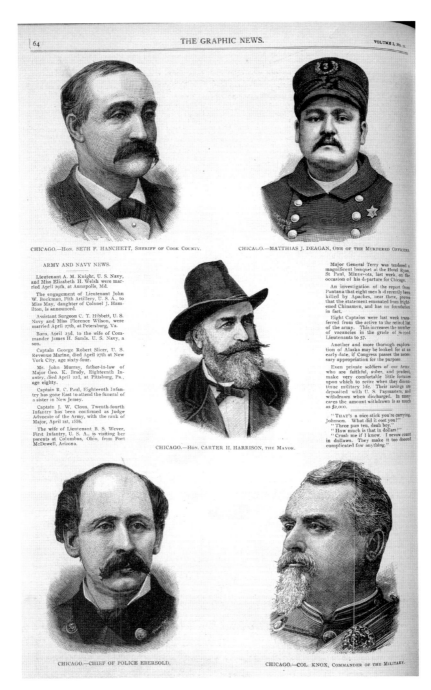

Officer Mathias Degan, et al. *Courtesy of the Chicago History Museum.*

First row, left to right: Officer Mathias Degan's badge. Officer John J. Barrett's badge. Officer George F. Miller's badge.

Middle row, left to right: Officer Timothy J. Flavin's badge. Officer Michael Sheehan's badge. Officer Thomas Redden's badge.

Third row, left to right: Officer Nels Hansen's badge. Officer Timothy Sullivan's badge. *All courtesy of the Chicago History Museum.*

The Policemen's Memorial
and the Badges of the Fallen Officers

"I command you in the name of the people of the State of Illinois to immediately and peaceably disperse."[74]

These were the words (tragically ironic) spoken by Captain William Ward at the head of the procession of police officers who marched up from the Desplaines Street Police Station as he and Inspector John Bonfield approached the speakers' wagon around 10:15 p.m. on the night of May 4. The nearly 180 police officers were organized in two columns of seven companies, with 18 to 25 officers per company. Ward and Bonfield led the men. Several of the lieutenants testified to the formation, where they stopped in the street, what Ward had said, Fielden's response ("We are peaceable."), the arched path of the bomb and the number of dead and wounded in their respective companies. Notice in the photos provided that there are seven officers who had died by the time of the trial. The eighth man, Timothy Sullivan, did not succumb to his wounds until almost two years later and, therefore, wasn't accounted for in the lieutenants' testimonies of the dead.

As mentioned earlier, there is little agreement in the testimony of either group of witnesses, prosecution or defense. This, I suspect, has less to do with dishonesty and more to do with the common human occurrence of flawed memory, especially in times of high stress and incredible trauma. Some details are consistent, though, from both groups of witnesses: the times of the meeting, the speeches, the marching of the officers from the station and the bomb being thrown. But there is little corroboration about the direction from where the bomb came, whether the explosion happened prior to gunfire, the gunfire prior to the bomb detonating or the simultaneity of them both. Questions remain as to whether Fielden or anyone else said, "Here come the bloodhounds! I'll do my duty, you do yours"; whether Fielden fired at the police; whether someone tried to use the incident to kill Spies. (His brother Heinrich was wounded as he stood next to August.)

The simple fact that there are so many stories—not even including the contradictory accounts of the reporters who were there with varied vantage points of the street that night—highlights the chaos and confusion of an event that most can only imagine. So, again we must lean on the more objective, scientifically based evidence that was submitted, as has been mentioned earlier: the testimony of the hardware store owner about the markings left in the street from the bomb, the direction of the bullet wounds in the officers, the composition of the shrapnel from the bomb compared to the composition of what was found in Lingg's room and around the city afterward. This doesn't even include the documented instances through newspaper accounts, city records and testimony of the tensions that existed in the city at that time and earlier between the largely immigrant groups of workers and the police.

History is about objectivity and honesty—as much as we can muster, admittedly, but striving to be as objective and honest as possible. The Policemen's Memorial and the display of the fallen officers' badges show at least one objective, honest result of the bombing: one is moved, I think, standing in front of display cases with the badges of those who have died in the line of duty, no matter what one's political bent or economic background is. The fact that there are men and women of varied ethnic and racial stripe who risk their lives for the greater good should cause us to stand in some sort of respectful gratitude. To deny this is simply naïve.

The statue stands in Bronzeville, on the southwest corner of 35th Street and Michigan Avenue (3510 South Michigan) in the back courtyard of Central Police Headquarters. The 1889 statue that originally stood in Haymarket Square was moved here and rededicated in 2007. Not many other statues or memorials to an event elicit such contrary views and emotions as does this one. From the time of its unveiling, it has stood as a rock solid testimony to courage, self-sacrifice, steadfastness and a "You shall go no further!" attitude that has tried to keep the social order as peaceful and ordered as possible. At the same time, for many, it stands as a symbol of a ruling class's power to keep the downtrodden trodden down.

Almost immediately after the dedication, ridicule was heaped on the memorial when the story circulated about the drunkenness of the officer who served as the model for the sculptor. About forty years later, an angered streetcar driver deliberately rammed his carriage into the statue in an explosion of disgust at the object's "command" to stop. The violence of the late 1960s spilled over one year after Chicago hosted a very contentious Democratic National Convention: an offshoot of the Students for a Democratic Society, the Weather Underground, detonated a bomb at the statue's base. After the second bombing on the same date in 1970, the statue was moved to the Police Academy and is now located at police headquarters. It's visible from the street but can be viewed up close by requesting admission to the courtyard through the main lobby.

The Police Officers' Memorial Statue. *Courtesy of Nathanael Filbert.*

The tenacity to display the statue, as well as its very survival since its creation, is a powerful symbol in and of itself. Inside the headquarters are the display cases of the badges of the eight officers killed in the Haymarket bombing (Display Case Section A-2), as well as the badges of all Chicago officers killed in the line of duty. There is also a display case, on the far side of the lobby toward the doors leading to the courtyard, that serves as an archive of those of the eight officers whose family members joined police forces in the city and surrounding areas.

It's unrealistic to think that we, today, are very much different from citizens of the late nineteenth century. We have similar dreams and fears, loves and suspicions. Society is still in need of the same protections against a lawless element that seeks to satisfy its self-serving appetites. Crime and political corruption are with us in the twenty-first century as they were then. In a culture as drenched as ours in such senseless violence and lawlessness, it is comforting to have a refuge for public safety. The police do provide this until that day when we, freely ordered, can live in peace without the coercion to do it.

THE HAYMARKET CEMETERY (OR MARTYRS') MEMORIAL AND GRAVE SITE

Tremble, tyrants and traitors…

Against you we are all soldiers
If they fall, our young heroes
France will bear new ones
Ready to join the fight against you…

Drive on sacred patriotism
Support our avenging arms
Liberty, cherished liberty
Join the struggle with your defenders
Under our flags, let victory
Hurry to your manly tone
So that in death your enemies
See your triumph and our glory![75]

These lyrics, at the closing of "The Marseillaise," France's national anthem, were the inspiration for the bronze statue that fronts the resting place of seven of the eight Haymarket men. The large monument portrays a statue of a woman standing over a fallen man, crowning him with the laurel wreath of victory. It's also referred to as the Haymarket Martyrs' Memorial by those who are sympathetic to the workers' cause. In 1998, the memorial was granted National Landmark status with all pomp and ceremony expected—and some show of the unexpected but not inappropriate. A group of Anarchists staged a protest to the government's sanctioning of the spot—in their view, usurping the memory, blood and voices of the men who are buried there. The sweet breath of liberty still exists!

Again, depending on perspective, one can see this as hijacking sacred memory along the lines (to some) of putting up a gift shop at the concentration camp at Auschwitz in Poland or a food court in Rome's Circus Maximus, site of first-century Christian executions. (I exaggerate for effect, of course.) But another way to see the reality is as a very belated acknowledgment by the government of an incident and the people who have been a part of it—the foundational event of greater social equity that still awaits full realization.

When the bodies of Parsons, Spies, Engel, Fischer and Lingg were released to their families and comrades (Lingg's body, because he was the sole member of his family to come to the United States, was given over to the Engels), the city allowed for Milwaukee Avenue to serve as the passageway for the funeral procession on Sunday, November 13. Beginning in Wicker Park, the body of each of the five men was brought out and added to the throng, estimated at over five thousand by newspaper accounts at the gathering and swelling to over ten thousand by the time the bodies reached the railroad yard for the cemetery trip.[76]

Police guards were stationed at the entrance of each of the houses, and incidents against them were limited to verbal ridicule by a few in the crowd and members of some of the dead men's families. There were no instances of violence or arrests reported. One *Times* reporter commented on the overall peaceful attitude of the crowd when a man, dressed in an army uniform ("Grand Army of the Republic" was the description given, so possibly a Union veteran of the Civil War), waved an American flag and cheered as the bodies passed him on Madison. He got a "feeble" echo from about six others, and the flag was withdrawn. The reporter had to admit that it was in bad taste.

The procession continued down Desplaines, about two blocks from where the bombing occurred, turned down Lake to cross the river and then down Wells to pass the offices of the *Arbeiter-Zeitung* and the *Alarm* until it got to the Wisconsin Central Railroad Depot around Harrison and LaSalle Streets in what is today Printers Row. Fifteen train cars were loaded with the bodies and packed with mourners to begin the final leg of the trip to the cemetery in Forest Park. A second train had to be gotten to accommodate the crowds.

At the cemetery, watched by dozens of police officers and quoted by reporters, four speakers proudly and unabashedly proclaimed words of hope and rebellion. Captain William Black, the chief defense attorney, quoted Jesus (but mixed stories) when he told the gathered, "Through eighteen centuries and more that loyal, that glorious one of Nazareth, to the question, 'What is Truth?' was in these words, 'I am the Truth.'" Robert Reitzel of Detroit spoke next and ended his remarks with, "We have loved long enough; let us at last hate."

All across the country, even in Europe, funeral services, protest rallies and violence occurred throughout the weekend. Peaceful events

The burial of five of the Haymarket men. *Courtesy of the Chicago History Museum.*

were reported from Denver to New York and everywhere in between. Preachers, also, weighed in on the events of the previous year on the Day of Rest when the burials happened—most turning the experience on the table of justice and social order. Trafalgar Square reported the bloodiest demonstrations as stories covering the all-day protests in London arrived early after the burials, appearing in Chicago's newspapers the next morning.

The memorial and grave site are at Forest Home Cemetery (originally called Waldheim Cemetery) in Forest Park, just south of I-290 (Eisenhower Expressway), about one block south of the Blue Line Forest Park station on Desplaines Avenue (not the City of Chicago's street of the same name). One enters the cemetery at the main entrance and follows the main road past the office building. At the left fork in the road, the grand statue is visible near the stone chapel, just to the right of it. Spies, Parsons, Engel, Fischer and Lingg were buried there on November 13, 1887. Schwab and Neebe would be buried there after their deaths in 1898 and 1916, respectively; Fielden died in Colorado in 1922 and is buried in that state.

Money was raised for a monument as well as for the material good of the family members of the executed and imprisoned by the Pioneer Aid and Support Association. The care of the monument and grave has since passed to the Illinois Labor History Society.

The memorial was dedicated on June 25, 1893, unveiled by Albert Parsons Jr. in the midst of a similar crowd to that which had gathered almost seven years before. The day after the dedication, Governor John Peter Altgeld issued his pardon of Fielden, Schwab and Neebe.

TWO EARS, ONE MOUTH

I n 1940, as Nazi bombs were falling all around him, George Orwell wrote:

> *England is a family with the wrong members in control....[We] are governed by the rich, and by people who step into positions of command by right of birth....Quite apart from anything else, the rule of money sees to it that we shall be governed largely by the old—that is by people utterly unable to grasp what age they are living in or what enemy they are fighting.*[77]

So has gone the march of history. Orwell observed the dire straits of 1939–40 England as Hitler's Blitz was slashing and burning the continent and its inhabitants and trying to spread it across the English Channel. The story of humanity is a series of dramas, tragedies, farces and comedic opera—a long train of endeavors to coexist on the same orbiting boulder that goes back to the darkest cave millennia ago. Orwell's experience of it is merely an ink spot on the parchment of the human record.

And our experience is similar. Perspective is the very limited ability to see what is now or what has been from our own vantage point. It's also the *in*ability to see the past or present from all sides. Objectivity is elusive, and it's unrealistic to act as if we possess it *in toto*—and it's unjust to hold those who think, look, believe, act differently than we do to a stricter standard of behavior and understanding. From one end of our existence, this striving for objectivity touches on the life of the academic who should strive for a historic truth that tells as full a story as possible, no matter what the topic.

On the other end of things is the more serious quest for peace in our day. The more we understand one another's origins, the more honestly we look at the past, the more open we keep ourselves to change, the closer we will be to true coexistence among anyone of any background, color, tax bracket or religion.

The parallels of history and contemporary times are not new. The Romans should have been prepared for their fifth-century final crumble by reading what others had said about the greats of their not-so-ancient past, the Roman Republic, Greece and Egypt. The civil authorities should not have been as surprised at what happened at the Haymarket because of their immediate history, remembered firsthand by many of them. And we should not be so baffled by the social ills that plague us in urban centers, conflicts with authority and even global threats to our individual lives. We need to look at these events and see where they have happened before. "There is nothing new under the sun" is not simply a biblical platitude. It's genuine historical reality: all things are repetitive. True, names, faces, languages, places may change, but the root issues are not new. To understand this is key to being better equipped to solve the major problems today.

The best we can do, and this is where peaceful coexistence can blossom, is to strive for mutual understanding. We temper our egos, subvert our self-interest, contravene our pride and curb our tongues so that listening can happen better. We have two ears and one mouth for a reason.

Listening better, we'll be better able to address the real issues of our day, not simply wax foolish about policies that are meaningless to a mother who has a dying baby strapped to her back waiting in line for a bowl of rice and a bottle of clean water and are actually damning to us as we ponder in the aisle of an overstocked grocery store what percentage of milk fat our bodies can take this week.

A free society of free human beings can exist only after the global social issues of past and present are addressed: poverty, lack of education, unemployment, automation and digitization at the expense of human labor, ongoing threats to human dignity at all its stages, prison systems that demand retribution rather than offering rehabilitation, anti-immigrant practices and the ever-growing tensions between public safety and personal liberty. And they need to be addressed by people other than the ever-present, self-serving Hydras we continue to elect and reelect and who continue to suck lifeblood from the weak and strangle humanity's progress. And to say, as August Spies said seconds before he was executed, "The day will come when our silence will be more powerful than the voices you are throttling today."

The Haymarket grave site. *Courtesy of Nathanael Filbert.*

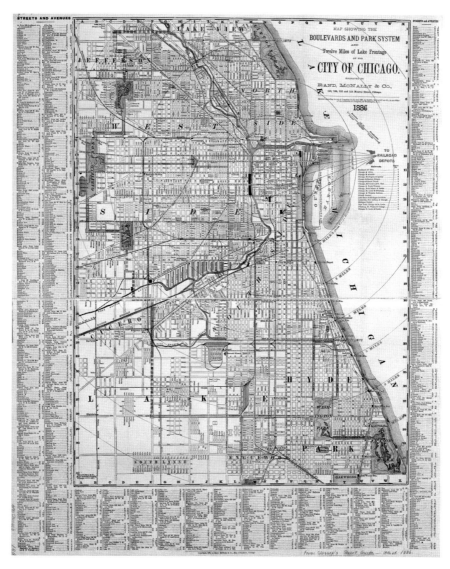

Chicago, 1886. *Courtesy of the Chicago History Museum.*

ADDITIONAL SITES[78]

For a more expansive experience, to see other places such as the homes of the eight or sites where their homes stood, sites related to the trial testimony (referenced by HADC ["Haymarket Affair Digital Collection"]) or the sites related to the historical background of this book, use this section. The addresses have been converted from the pre-1909 numbering system to the present ones.[79]

August Spies's homes: *2132 West Potomac and 620 Park

Albert and Lucy Parsonses' homes: *1374 West Grand and *1120 Grand

Site of Adolph Fischer's home: 1336 North Dean (near Milwaukee and Paulina)

Site of George Engel's home: 960–62 North Milwaukee (Kennedy Expressway)

Site of Godfried Waller's home: between 835 and 843 North Milwaukee (Kennedy Expressway)

Site of Samuel Fielden's home: 543 West Polk (near Polk and South Canal Street)

Site of Michael Schwab's home: 226 Florimond Street

Site of Oscar Neebe's home: 723 West Roosevelt

Site of Mayor Carter Harrison Sr.'s home: between 306 and 316 South Ashland

Site of State's Attorney Julius Grinnell's home: 530 Aldine Square

Site of the offices of attorneys Salomon & Zeisler: between 536 and 638 North LaSalle

Site of the office of attorney William P. Black: 603 North Dearborn

Site of Chicago Avenue Police Station: 113 West Chicago

Site of the Grand Pacific Hotel: northeast corner of Jackson and LaSalle

Cache of bombs found: corner of Damen (formerly Robey) and Bloomingdale (see HADC, Volume K, 661–64)

Site of the Relief and Aid Society: northeast corner of LaSalle and Randolph

Site of the original Cook County Courthouse: corner of Clark and Randolph

(Old) St. Patrick's Church: *northwest corner of Desplaines and Adams

*Denotes still standing

Cemetery Residents

Forest Home (Forest Park, Illinois)

George Engel
Adolph Fischer
Emma Goldman
Louis Lingg
Meta Neebe
Oscar Neebe
Albert Parsons
Lucy Parsons
Michael Schwab
August Spies

Graceland
(Clark Street and Irving Park Road)

John Peter Altgeld
Phillip Armour
Richard Teller Crane
Marshall Field
Carter Harrison Sr.

Cyrus McCormick Jr.
Cyrus McCormick Sr.
Joseph Medill
Potter and Bertha Palmer
Allan Pinkerton
George Pullman

ROSEHILL (RAVENSWOOD IN BETWEEN PETERSON AND BRYN MAWR)

Levi Boone
Roswell Mason

ST. BONIFACE (CLARK STREET AND LAWRENCE STREET)

Mathias Degan

CHRONOLOGY

(To provide more context, some time markers for other events not mentioned in the book have been included.)

1673: Louis Joliet enters the area around a lake and a river, later to be known as Chicago.

1775–81: The American Revolution is fought.

1776: July 4: The thirteen colonies along the Atlantic seaboard declare their independence from the British Empire.

1777: The Articles of Confederation are adopted as the governing body of law for the newly created nation.

1787: September 17: The Constitution of the United States is created to replace the Articles of Confederation as the legal guide for the country. It is ratified by the majority of delegates the following year.

1790: Jean Baptiste Point du Sable becomes the first nonnative, non–tax paying resident.

1803: Fort Dearborn is built on the south bank of the Chicago River, near its mouth.

1812–14: The War of 1812 is fought. In the first year of the conflict, the Battle of Fort Dearborn (the Fort Dearborn Massacre) results in the temporary loss of the fort by U.S. troops at the hands of the Native American allies of the British.

1837: The city of Chicago is incorporated.

1846–48: The Mexican-American War is fought.

1848: "The Springtime of the Peoples," popular uprisings, erupt in almost a dozen nations and empires throughout western and central Europe, with the result of a large number of immigrants coming to the United States.

1855: The "Lager Beer Riot" breaks out at the courthouse on Clark and Randolph Streets.

1860: Abraham Lincoln is nominated as the Republican Party's candidate for president.

1861–65: The American Civil War is fought.

1865: April 14: President Abraham Lincoln is shot at Ford's Theatre in Washington, D.C., and dies the next morning.

1866–67: Eight-hour workday legislation is passed and nullified in Illinois.

1871: The Chicago Fire blazes.

1872–73: The "Bread Riot" erupts at the Relief and Aid Society building at LaSalle and Randolph.

1877: The Railroad Strike sweeps across the country east of the Mississippi River.

1881: President James Garfield is assassinated in Washington, D.C.

1883: *The Pittsburgh Manifesto* is promulgated at the International Working People's Association gathering.

1884: The first "Poor People's March" occurs on Thanksgiving Day.

1885: April: The new building for the Chicago Board of Trade opens at LaSalle and Jackson.

May: Victor Hugo dies.

July: The "Streetcar Workers' Strike" occurs over the summer.

November: The second Thanksgiving Day "Poor People's March" takes place.

1886: February: Strikes and lockouts begin in Chicago at McCormick Reaper Works, Maxwell Brothers' Box Making, Deering Manufacturing, Couhour and Cummings Nail Mill, Lichtenstadt Brick Manufacturing and Nussbaumer Cigar Manufacturing.

May 1: The national strike for the eight-hour workday begins. Upward of 350,000 workers across the country—at least 65,000 in Chicago—walk off their jobs.

May 3: Violence breaks out at the McCormick Reaper Works as August Spies addresses striking lumber workers near the factory.

May 3: The "Monday Night Conspiracy Meeting" is held at Grief's Hall.

May 4: The bomb explodes at the Haymarket meeting.

May 5: Mass arrests, searches and suspensions of gatherings are ordered in Chicago.

June 21: The Haymarket trial begins. Jury selection opens.

July 15: Jury selection concludes and testimony begins.

August 11: The trial concludes and the jury begins deliberation.

August 20: The jury reaches a guilty verdict. Execution is set for December 3.

November 26: The Illinois Supreme Court agrees to hear the appeal.

Dyer Lum's *A Concise History of the Great Trial of the Chicago Anarchists in 1886* is published.

1887: March 4: The appeal begins.

September 14: The conviction is upheld and execution is set for November 11.

November 2: The U.S. Supreme Court denies a hearing of the case.

November 10: Fielden and Schwab are granted commuted sentences to life in prison.

November 10: Lingg commits suicide.

November 11: Spies, Parsons, Engel and Fischer are executed.

November 13: The five dead men are processed down Milwaukee Avenue, through downtown and to Forest Home Cemetery for burial.

1888–93: The Clemency Movement works for the release of Fielden, Schwab and Neebe.

1889: May 1: May Day is celebrated in Paris for Republican France's 100th birthday.

May 30: The Police Memorial is dedicated at Haymarket Square.

1890: Chicago is awarded the honor of hosting the World's Fair in 1893. It's at this time that the city wins the renowned nickname "Windy City" for its politicians' ability to blow a lot of air about Chicago's greatness.

1891: Pope Leo XIII publishes *Rerum Novarum*, the first major statement of organized religion defining social responsibilities of capital and labor as a vehicle for a more just society.

1893: May–October: The World's Columbian Exposition (the World's Fair) is held in Chicago with over twenty-three million visitors from around the world.

June 25: The Haymarket Memorial is dedicated at Forest Home Cemetery.

June 26: Governor Altgeld pardons Fielden, Schwab and Neebe.

October 28: Mayor Carter Harrison is assassinated.

1894: Eugene Victor Debs is arrested and sentenced to a six-month prison term for leading the Pullman Porter Strike, defying a federal injunction.

1898: April–August: The Spanish-American War is fought.

Michael Schwab dies.

1900: Eugene Debs runs for the office of president of the United States as the Socialist candidate in the elections of 1900, 1904, 1908 and 1912. In 1920, he becomes the only candidate to run for that office from prison.

1905: The Industrial Workers of the World is established at the Continental Congress of the Working Class in Chicago.

1914–18: The First World War is fought.

1916: Oscar Neebe dies.

1917: February–November: The Russian Revolution topples centuries of tsarist rule and claims the birth of a workers' paradise.
  April: The United States enters World War I.

1918: Eugene Debs is arrested and sentenced to ten years in prison for publicly condemning American participation in World War I. President Warren G. Harding commutes his sentence to time served in 1921.

1919: Eugene Williams is killed after swimming in a "whites only" area of beach at Lake Michigan. The murder sparks several days of rioting, leaving thirty-eight dead.

1922: Samuel Fielden dies.

1926: Eugene Debs dies.

1932: "The Bonus Army" marches on Washington, D.C., forty-three thousand strong (seventeen thousand World War I vets and their families) to demand the added pay they were promised for serving in the American Expeditionary Force in Europe during the "Great War."

1936: Henry David's *The History of the Haymarket Affair* is published.

1938: The Fair Labor Standards Act is passed, mandating, by the federal government, maximum workweek hours, overtime pay and restrictions on child labor.

1939–45: The Second World War is fought.

1941: The United States enters World War II.

1950–53: The Korean War is fought.

1955–75: The Vietnam War is fought.

1963: November 22: President John Kennedy is assassinated in Dallas, Texas.

1968: April: Dr. Martin Luther King Jr. is assassinated in Memphis, Tennessee.

May: The Illinois Labor History Society holds a rally at Randolph and Desplaines Streets, accelerating the process of recognition of the site's historical significance.

August: Protests at the Democratic National Convention at Grant Park result in brutal confrontations between protesters, police and the National Guard.

1969 and 1970: The Police Memorial is blown up by members of the Weather Underground, an offshoot of the Students for a Democratic Society. It was repaired after both incidents, eventually moved in 1972 and then in 2007 to its present location at 35th and Michigan.

1984: Paul Avrich's *The Haymarket Tragedy* is published.

1986: Mayor Harold Washington gives support for a memorial park at the Haymarket site.

1989: The revolutions of 1989 spread across Eastern and Central Europe as popular protests grow.

November 9: Citizens of Berlin begin to demolish the wall that had split the city since 1961.

1991: December: The Soviet Union officially reverts to its pre-Communist name of Russia, sans a huge bulk of territory claimed by fourteen of its former republics-turned-independent-nations.

Pope John Paul II publishes *Centesimus Annus*, reaffirming Christian social teaching on the 100th anniversary of Leo XIII's groundbreaking encyclical "On Capital and Labor."

1993: The World Trade Center is bombed for the first time.

1997: The U.S. Parks Service designates the Haymarket Memorial in Forest Home Cemetery a national landmark.

2001: September 11: The World Trade Center is destroyed, the Pentagon is damaged and a plane believed destined for the White House crashes in a field in Pennsylvania, resulting in nearly three thousand deaths.

2006: James Green's *Death in the Haymarket* is published.

2007: September 14: The Haymarket Memorial Statue, created by Mary Brogger, is dedicated on the site where the speakers' wagon stood at Randolph and Desplaines the night of the bombing.

2010: "The Arab Spring" sweeps across several countries of North Africa, instituting changes in some of the governments in the region.

The Chicago History Museum completes the Haymarket Affair Digital Collection, making the complete trial transcripts and related material easily accessible for the first time.

2011: The Occupy Movement, inspired in part by civil protests in North Africa the year before, spreads from Wall Street to many major cities throughout the world in an uncoordinated but unified cry for political and economic accountability and reform.

Timothy Messer-Kruse's *The Trial of the Haymarket Anarchists* is published.

2012: Timothy Messer-Kruse's *The Haymarket Conspiracy* is published.

2014: August 9: Violence breaks out after the death of Michael Brown in Ferguson, Missouri, and continues through the rest of the summer and into the following years in various urban centers in the country, including Chicago.

October 14: Laquan McDonald is killed by police.

2015: November 24: Protests are staged in Chicago and throughout the country after surveillance video is released showing McDonald being shot sixteen times in a thirteen-second period. The protests continue into the winter and spring.

2016: April 13: Mayor Rahm Emanuel's Task Force on Police Accountability releases its report.

NOTES

Chapter 1

1. For the purposes of this work, I use the general definition for the philosophies mentioned in the book. So, generally, for the principles of socialism: this is the belief that the ownership and workings of the means of production are controlled by all members of society and that the fruits of it are shared by all. For anarchism, it is the belief that any form of government is coercive and therefore undesirable. For capitalism, it is the system whereby the means of production and distribution of goods are privately owned and managed to maximize profit. These are broad definitions meant only to give minimal clarification and admitting that the nineteenth-century reality allowed wide interpretation.
2. I found the introduction of Messer-Kruse's book particularly helpful in laying out the many issues to be addressed on this topic. Messer-Kruse, *Trial of the Haymarket Anarchists*, 1–8.
3. Haymarket Affair Digital Collection, Chicago Historical Society, Jury Selection: Court Discussion, Vol. C, 184–8 (particularly 186–88).
4. *Chicago Daily Tribune*, "Nearly 1,000 Examined," July 16, 1886, 1.

Chapter 3

5. www.censusrecords.net/cities/chicago_census.html.
6. *Chicago Daily Tribune*, "Prohibitory Liquor Law," April 25, 1855, 1.

7. Brady and Hogan, *Great Chicago Beer Riot*, 75–82.

8. *Chicago Daily Tribune*, "Prohibitory Liquor Law," April 25, 1885, 1.

9. www.measuringworth.com, using the "GDP" Deflator calculation.

10. Nelson, *Chicago Relief and Aid Society*.

11. *Chicago Daily Tribune*, "The Unemployed," December 23, 1873, 1.

12. Ibid.

13. Ibid., July 20, 1877, 4.

14. Ibid., "The Death Roll," July 29, 1877, 10.

15. *Chicago Times*, "Red Riot," July 18, 1877, 2; *Chicago Times*, "Terror's Reign," July 26, 1877, 1; *Chicago Daily News*, "Progress of the Riot," July 24, 1877, 5:00 p.m. Extra, 1.

16. *Chicago Times*, "Woman's Part in the Riots," July 27, 1877, 2.

17. Ibid., "Mob Menace," July 27, 1877, 1.

18. Ibid., "Law or Labor?," July 25, 1877, 9.

19. *Chicago Daily Tribune*, "The Great Strike," July 22, 1877, 1.

20. Bruce, *1877: Year of Violence*, 44–65.

21. *Chicago Socialist*, "The Trade Dollar," September 14, 1878, 2.

22. Drury, *Manifesto of the International Working People's Association*, 1–9.

23. *Chicago Times*, "And the Tramps, Too" and "The Red Flag," November 27, 1884, 8.

24. www.measuringworth.com, using the "CPI" calculation.

25. *Daily Inter Ocean*, April 29, 1885, 8.

26. Haymarket Affair Digital Collection, Chicago Historical Society, Witness Testimony, Vol. J, Testimony of Marshall H. Williamson, 6–15.

27. *Chicago Daily News*, "Bloodshed at Lamont," May 4, 1885, 5:00 p.m. Edition, 1.

28. Ibid., "More Bloodshed Feared," May 25, 1885, 1; *Chicago Daily News*, "Victor Hugo Laid to Rest," June 1, 1885, 1.

29. *Chicago Daily Tribune*, "Tramp, Tramp, Tramp," July 1, 1885, 1.

30. Ibid., 2.

31. *Chicago Daily News*, "Streetcar Men's Strike," June 30, 1885, 1.

32. Ibid., "Using Force," July 1, 1885, 1.

33. Ibid.

34. This chronology is set out in *Chicago Daily News*, "A Lively Time," July 2, 1885, 2.

35. *Chicago Daily News*, "The Cars Were Run," July 3, 1885, 1.

36. *Chicago Daily Tribune*, "No Bloodshed," July 7, 1885, 1.

37. Ibid., "The Cars Were Run: Mayor Harrison," July 4, 1885, 1.

38. *Chicago Daily News*, "The Cars Were Run," July 3, 1885, 1.

39. *Chicago Daily Tribune*, "Will Try Again," July 6, 1885, 1.

40. Ibid., "No Bloodshed," July 7, 1885, 1–2.

41. Ibid., "Everything Lovely: Anarchists Down on the Men," July 9, 1885, 2.

42. Haymarket Affair Digital Collection, Chicago Historical Society, Witness Testimony, Vol. N, 20ff.

43. For a full account of the evidence supporting the conspiracy charge as well as the testimony connecting Lingg to the actual bomb used at the rally, see the Haymarket Affair Digital Collection, Chicago Historical Society, Witness Testimony, Vol. K, and Proceedings of the Illinois Supreme Court, Vol. O.

44. The wages for workers of various trades were gleaned from references in Chicago's daily papers in stories about labor issues in the spring and summer of 1886.

45. Reading the transcripts of the selection process, the defense's writ of errors submitted to the Illinois Supreme Court after the guilty verdict was passed and the Supreme Court's reasons for not granting the appeal, one gains a clearer understanding of what actually happened. The details are far outside the scope of this work. Timothy Messer-Kruse's *Trial of the Haymarket Anarchists* is the best source for further study.

46. See the Haymarket Affair Digital Collection, Chicago Historical Society, People's Exhibits 16–128, particularly #s16, 22 and 31.

47. For a sample of the tone of late nineteenth-century newspaper editorializing, see Chicago Times, "Murderers Arrested" and "Raiding Rat-Holes," May 6, 1886, 1; "Clubs Are Trumps," July 3, 1885, 1–2. From the *Chicago Tribune*, July 20, 1877, 4; July 26, 1877; "Pitched Battles!," July 27, 1877, 1; July 28, 1877, 1. From the *Chicago Daily News*, July 17, 1877, "The Great Strike," 1; July 23, 1877, Victor Lawson's editorial, 2; July 24, 1877, "The Insurrection," 1. Granted, this is but a small sample; a treatment of the issue of editorial bias is beyond the scope of this work.

48. *Chicago Times*, "Law Supreme," November 12, 1887, 1ff.

49. Thanks go to Dr. Bernard Brandon Scott, formerly of St. Meinrad School of Theology, for the quotation and, more importantly, for the understanding that this quote elicits.

Chapter 4

50. www.illinoislaborhistory.org, "Haymarket Memorial Dedicated."

51. For a thorough breakdown of the shrapnel and bullet wounds, see Messer-Kruse, *Trial of the Haymarket Anarchists*, "The Elements of a Riot," 99–107; and the Haymarket Affair Digital Collection, Chicago Historical Society, Witness Testimony, Vol. K, 99–104, 551–73, 617–19, 640–45, 691–97; Vol. L, 221–66.

52. For a full account of the location of the bomb thrower and Metzner's observations and testimony, see Messer-Kruse, *Trial of the Haymarket Anarchists*, 110–16.

53. See Haymarket Affair Digital Collection, Chicago Historical Society, Post-Testimony Discourse, Vol. O, 2.

54. Ibid., Witness Testimony, Vol. K, 405ff.

55. Ibid., Witness Testimony, Vol. K, 551–73, 617–19, 640–45, 691–97.

56. See Green, *Death in the Haymarket*, "A Night of Terror," 190–91, for a summation of the newspaper accounts of civilian casualties in the days after the bombing.

57. See Haymarket Affair Digital Collection, Chicago Historical Society, Witness Testimony, Vol. N, 134.

58. Messer-Kruse, *Trial of the Haymarket Anarchists*, "The Prosecution," 55–75.

59. The Chicago History Museum has the circulars from the period on display. Check them out as well as the whole span of this cut of Chicago history.

60. See www.gpo.gov, "4th Amendment: Search and Seizure," 1205. There are two case references that I found helpful: the first is *Boyd v. US*, 116 U.S. 616, 627 (1886), which was contemporary to our study. In this case, the defendant's right to non-self-incrimination due to evidence seized was upheld. The evidence was a collection of personal financial records. The second case, a generation after the Haymarket events, *Adams v. NY*, 192 U.S. 585, 598 (1904), dealt with evidence seized in direct violation of New York gaming law. Though it was judged after the events of this book, it's beneficial to see the consistency of defending civic order (be it gambling or revolution) over an individual's personal rights.

61. Messer-Kruse's treatment of the conspiracy issue takes the Market Square into account; see *Trial of the Haymarket Anarchists*, "The Prosecution," 59–60.

62. For a sample of more of the editorial attitudes of the period, see *Chicago Tribune*, "The Mass-Meeting," July 24, 1877, 4; "Police Headquarters," "Parsons," "The Abortive Meeting," et al., July 26, 1877; and *Chicago Times*, "Law Supreme," May 6, 1886, 1ff.

63. See Haymarket Affair Digital Collection, Chicago Historical Society, People's Exhibits 15–128 (except Exhibit 62) for all the articles submitted by the prosecution.

64. Ibid., Witness Testimony, Vol. M, 134.

65. Ibid., Petition for Change of Venue, Vol. I, 23–24.

66. *Chicago Daily Tribune*, "A Strong Stay Snapped," July 16, 1886, 1.

67. See Haymarket Affair Digital Collection, Chicago Historical Society, Witness Testimony, Vol. K, 639–40.

68. Messer-Kruse, *Trial of the Haymarket Anarchists*, "Executions and Amnesty," 153–56.

69. *Chicago Daily Tribune*, "Nearly 1,000 Examined," July 16, 1886, 1.

70. See Haymarket Affair Digital Collection, Chicago Historical Society, Examination of Jurors, Vol. A, 56–61.

71. William Seliger gave the entirety of his and Lingg's movements of May 4 in his testimony on July 21. See the Haymarket Affair Digital Collection, Chicago Historical Society, Witness Testimony, Vol. I, 506–46.

72. See Haymarket Affair Digital Collection, Chicago Historical Society, Witness Testimony, Vol. K, 582–83, 637 and 661–64.

73. Ibid., The Accused, the Accusers: The Famous Speeches of the Eight Chicago Anarchists in Court When Asked If They Had Anything to Say Why Sentence Should Not Be Passed Upon Them, October 7th, 8th, and 9th, 1886, Address of Louis Lingg, 42.

74. Ibid., Witness Testimony, Vol. I, 22–25.

75. www.marseillaise.org, "La Marseillaise—English Lyrics."

76. See *Chicago Daily Times*, "Laid at Rest," November 14, 1887, 1ff, for a narrative of the events through the close of the graveside service as well as the memorials, rallies and other incidents around the country and world.

Epilogue

77. Orwell, "Lion and the Unicorn," 54–55.

Additional Sites

78. Throughout Professor William J. Adelman's book *Haymarket Revisited*, he cites these places of interest that could be visited. I add them in at the end of the text to aid further exploration.

79. See *Plan of Re-numbering City of Chicago*.

Annotated Bibliography of Sources Cited

Adelman, William J. *Haymarket Revisited: A Tour Guide of Labor History Sites and Ethnic Neighborhoods Connected with the Haymarket Affair.* **Chicago: Illinois Labor History Society, 1986.**
Though meandering, clunky at times and decidedly one-sided, this is a most detailed tour book and the only one related to the Haymarket events of which I'm aware. I did the entire three-sectioned tour via my feet and the Chicago Transit Authority over a period of several days. The legwork that Adelman and his colleagues at the Illinois Labor History Society have done in the two editions (1976 and 1986) of the book has been invaluable to me. While a lot of the book is only distantly connected to the Haymarket Affair and outdated in sections, it provides a valuable archive for the racial and ethnic mix of Chicago's labor history. The work gave me my introduction to as close to a street-by-street familiarity with this city as I'll ever possess. If you have the extended time, get a copy and get to walking!

Aquino, Corinne. "Old Addresses." Forgotten Chicago, December 13, 2008. forgottenchicago.com/articles/oldaddresses.
This page answered my questions about the bizarre numbering in nineteenth-century Chicago. The whole "Forgotten Chicago" website is a treasure of writing and pictures about our past—both well-known and obscure. It's one of the best user-supported sites I've ever come across. The passion of people who have even a remote connection with this city is evident with almost every post from the past.

Berkowow. "The Labor Trail." Community Walk, 2013. communitywalk.com/map.
The trail is a great way to track the geographic highlights of Chicago's labor history. Each topic is seen as part of the whole as well as a zoomed-in piece of specific history. The website is part of my take-along travel brochure for future vacation spots around the country.

Brady, Judy E., and John F. Hogan. *The Great Chicago Beer Riot*. Charleston, SC: The History Press, 2015.
I found this book in a small bookstore downtown as I was along my many "just browsing" days off. While I cover the 1855 event only cursorily, reading this book gave me a fuller appreciation for this little-known event of Chicago's past. Brady and Hogan show how early prejudices and reactionary policies affect events that followed and affected them even into the next century.

Bruce, Robert V. *1877: Year of Violence*. Chicago: Ivan R. Dee, 1989.
A second edition, this work is an invaluable source for background material that paints a clear picture of the national labor scene in the decade following the Civil War that culminated in the "Great Uprising" and had such an impact for that generation in Chicago and around the country. Bruce's account and research is herculean in its scope and provides a full account of this too-unknown watershed time in American history.

Chicago Times. **Chicago History Museum, microfilm collection, May 1–3, 1886; November 1–30, 1887.**
Chicago Tribune. **Chicago History Museum, microfilm collection, July 1–31, 1877; June 30–July 31, 1885; May 1–August 31, 1886.**
Daily Inter Ocean. **Chicago History Museum, microfilm collection, March 1–April 30, 1885.**
These references to the daily newspapers of nineteenth-century Chicago represent many hours staring at computer screens and reading microfilm. The experience has been an unexpected gift as I perused the past, not simply for the topic at hand, but in my optical wanderings reading advertisements, cartoons and side stories of the day.

Drury, Victor, et al. *Manifesto of the International Working People's Association*. Haymarket Affair Digital Collection. Chicago Historical Society, Exhibits, People's Exhibit 19. *The Alarm*, November 1, 1884.

One of the most damning pieces of evidence entered by the prosecution, the manifesto of October 16, 1883, laid out a blueprint for social revolution as professed by its authors, among them Albert Parsons and August Spies. The plan makes a clear argument for the necessity to change the imbalance of the structure of society, albeit a radical one, and places the responsibility for this change in the hands of the worker since all other avenues had failed or were purposefully sabotaged.

Green, James R. *Death in the Haymarket: A Story of Chicago, the First Labor Movement, and the Bombing That Divided Gilded Age America*. New York: Pantheon, 2006.
While not having the whole of the trial transcripts accessible as we have them now, Green makes a clear presentation of his positions on the issues and effects of the events in the last century. I discovered this book in the Chicago History Museum's gift shop when I first moved here. It was inspirational to me to first visit the site at Randolph and Desplaines and got me interested in an idea for a stage play of the events. (Presently that idea is still on the back burner to allow me to see this work to completion.)

The Haymarket Affair Digital Collection. Chicago Historical Society.
This is the essential collection of documents related to the Haymarket Affair. The society's gathering and digitizing of the transcripts, appeal documents, the eight men's addresses to the court after their convictions, the newspaper editorials and the summaries/chronologies and photo collection are the best testament to the events for any e-ready generation to come. I spent almost a full year (April 2012–March 2013) reading the entire transcript, taking notes and outlining a dramatic (i.e. staged) tribute in my head. Somewhere in the midst of the tens of thousands of pages of trial drama, this book took shape. And again, the staff at the museum and the Research Center provided me with invaluable assistance, from those who uploaded the collection to the curators presently responsible for its upkeep.

Kendall. "The Lehr-und-Wehr Verein and the Second Amendment." Chicago Crime Scenes Project, July 8, 2009. chicagocrimescenes.blogspot.com.
More information than I was looking for, but it gave me the first photo I've seen of Neff's Hall. Sadly, in books and other sources covering the affair up to 2009, this photo is always absent. Granted, it's not a pretty building, but it's still part of the archive that needs to be recorded and preserved.

Measuring Worth. "Relative Worth." Measuringworth.com. 2013. This is a very helpful site with a variety of conversion tables to compare values of different amounts at different time periods. The site is monitored by a local man who appreciates knowing that the work is of benefit to advancing the historical record.

Messer-Kruse, Timothy. *The Haymarket Conspiracy: Transatlantic Anarchist Networks*. **Urbana: University of Illinois, 2012.** This work is an excellent follow-up and companion piece to the author's first book on the subject referenced below. It details and cites the organized theories and praxis of the nineteenth-century Anarchists. While a person can read one without the other, the topic is certainly better served when studied together. This work is a seamless sequel to his first book and will only help clarify the historical record.

————. *The Trial of the Haymarket Anarchists: Terrorism and Justice in the Gilded Age*. **New York: Palgrave Macmillan, 2011.** The seminal work of a long-overdue contemporary rethinking of the events that make up the Haymarket Affair, Messer-Kruse's first book on the topic inspired me to read the whole of the trial transcripts and related documents. He is balanced, honest and courageous even while being a tad iconoclastic in his insistence on rewriting what has been taken for granted for over 130 years. I admit it was a difficult tablet to swallow at first gulp but well worth the read for a more complete understanding of the subject than has ever been accomplished.

Nelson, Otto M. *The Chicago Relief and Aid Society, 1850–1874.* **N.p., n.d., 59–66.** *Journal of the Illinois State Historical Society (1908–1984)* **59, no. 1 (Spring 1966): 48–66. www.jstor.org.** This is a digitized version of a study summarizing the works of the Relief and Aid Society before the Chicago Fire and the three years after it. It's a thorough piece with photographs of the society's building, along with several officers of the society. It's become clear to me that the electronic preservation of records such as these has and will continue to assist researchers in more accurately telling the human story throughout all its chapters.

Officer Down Memorial Page. "End of Watch." Odmp.com. This is a dignified and touching tribute to all the Chicago Police Department officers who have died in service. The "end of watch" is the phrase used to mark their dates of death. This site was one of the first I discovered in my early research, and it gave me the cemetery where Mathias Degan, the first casualty of the bombing, is buried. Again, the police department is to be commended for its vigilance with this site as well as the displays and statue at the Central Police Headquarters.

Orwell, George. "The Lion and the Unicorn: Socialism and the English Genius." *Why I Write*. **New York: Penguin, 2005, 11–94.**
This work is essential for anyone seeking to understand or to further the ideas of Socialism (without Stalin's totalitarianism) and gain insight to its theories put into practice. The whole collection of essays is enlightening and enjoyable. Even more importantly, I think, is that he wrote this as a "call to arms" of sorts for the British people and government and the only way to come out of the Second World War victorious. Orwell's wit and creativity come out clearly in the piece. It, along with the other essays in the collection, is as relevant today as it was when bombs were dropping all over him.

Plan of Re-numbering City of Chicago; a Complete Table Showing New and Old Numbers Affected by an Ordinance Passed by the City Council of the City of Chicago, June 22, 1908, and as Amended by an Ordinance Passed June 21, 1909. **Chicago: Chicago Directory, 1909.**
This is one of the most valuable resources for anyone researching sites in Chicago before the 1909 renumbering of the addresses in the city. It is the complete table of conversion from the muddled system that was in use before the Burnham Plan to the user-friendly numbering of the grid system still in use today. While I still had to consult some tattered hard copies of Chicago directories from the 1880s and 1890s, the time saved with this downloadable table was pure gift.

United States Government Publishing Office. "Fourth Amendment: Search and Seizure." www.gpo.gov/fdsys/pkg/ GPO-CONAN-1992/pdf.
I had to bone up a bit on the elements of the freedom from illegal searches and seizures. The Government Publishing Office has kept pace well with technology in preserving the legal history of the nation, lest we forget.

Annotated Bibliography of Resources for Further Study

Avrich, Paul. *The Haymarket Tragedy*. Princeton, NJ: Princeton University Press, 1984.
This is one of the last of the Haymarket authors who did not have easy access to the trial transcripts as we do today. It was the premier book of its generation on the subject. It's cited a lot in books and articles on the subject but is limited now in the effort to reevaluate the events in the twenty-first century.

David, Henry. *The History of the Haymarket Affair*. New York: Farrar & Rinehart, 1936.
This is the earliest history of the events written in the twentieth century. As with the other historians prior to Messer-Kruse, David did not have the accessibility of the whole of the trial transcripts as we currently have them. The book has served as a guide for all research on the topic through the close of that century.

Foner, Phillip Sheldon, and W.P. Black. *The Autobiographies of the Haymarket Martyrs*. New York: Pathfinder, 1977.
This is the collection of the Haymarket Eight's autobiographies that seven of them wrote for a series in *The Knights of Labor*. They appeared from October 16, 1886, through March 5, 1887, as supporters worked for the appeal of the convictions. Louis Lingg's autobiography never appeared in the journal. Foner discovered his piece in issues of the *Alarm* from December 29, 1888,

through January 5, 1889, and, thankfully, included it in the latest edition of the collection. While they're autobiographical and not specifically objective history, they still retain value for the historical record in that they describe a particular time in American and European history and these men's attitudes about them, their world and themselves. They should be seen in the same light as other memoirs and diaries of the day.

Gilbert, Amos. *The Life of Thomas Skidmore*. **Chicago: Charles H. Kerr, 1984.**

This is a very short sketch of America's (and the planet's) first Socialist (1790–1832). It was originally written shortly after Thomas Skidmore's death. The pamphlet-style book is certainly not of the caliber or breadth of contemporary biographies, but it serves as a good introduction to a little-known political theorist, realizing that he predated and influenced Karl Marx.

Lanctot, Barbara. *A Walk Through Graceland Cemetery*. **Chicago: Chicago Architectural Foundation, 1988.**

This serves as a solid guide through the cemetery that houses several notables from Chicago's past who were involved either directly or indirectly in the Haymarket events. The book is set up to be used in a self-guided tour or as background information. Whether the book is used at the cemetery or not or whether a person utilizes the cemetery staff for a tour, a walk through the place is an enriching experience.

Lum, Dyer D. *A Concise History of the Great Trial of the Chicago Anarchists in 1886*. **Chicago: Socialist Pub. Society, 1886.**

This is the source from which all other histories of the events have been taken until our own time. As touched on earlier, Lum made the history out of the summary of the trial prepared by the defense team for the appeal to the Illinois Supreme Court. Messer-Kruse shows how this third-hand material being given status as a primary source has led many to their sometimes flawed, less-than-objective conclusions. It bears repeating that, for honest history to be done, a complete look at the record needs to happen. A critical look at Lum's work is essential in the effort.

Paine, Thomas. *Rights of Man*. **Edited by Ronald Herder. New York: Dover Publications, 1999.**

This was written in 1791 as a response to the condemnation, in England, of the French Revolution. Paine sets out the problems with monarchism and the benefits of representative democracy as was being played out in the newly constituted United States. The nineteenth-century Anarchists used Paine's work as part of the philosophical underpinning of the new world they sought to bring into being, replacing the monarchy of capitalism with a more equitable social system.

Parsons, Lucy E. *Life of Albert R. Parsons with a Brief History of the Labor Movement in America; Also Sketches of the Lives of A. Spies, Geo. Engel, A. Fischer and Louis Lingg*. **Chicago: L.E. Parsons, 1903.**
First published in 1889, this is as complete a collection of background material for one of the leading speakers for social and labor reform in late nineteenth-century Chicago as one will find. Also, it contains information on the others involved in the movement and Haymarket Affair, and coupled with other autobiographies published by the Knights of Labor, we have a large body of firsthand work by people who were directly involved in the movement and the events they produced.

Roediger, David, and Franklin Rosemont, eds. *Haymarket Scrapbook, 125th Anniversary Edition*. **Oakland, CA: AK Press, 2012.**
This is a valuable resource for reprints of primary source material of the eight men of Haymarket and other people's memories of them from around the world. The book is an impressive collection of articles, essays, memories, cartoons, sketches and photographs related to Haymarket and the movements that were inspired by it.

Rogovin, Mark, ed. *The Day Will Come: Honoring Our Working Class Heroes. Stories of the Haymarket Martyrs and the Dedicated Men and Women Buried Alongside the Monument*. **Chicago: Illinois Labor History Society, 2011. www.illinoislaborhistory. org/haymarket-tour-intro.html.**
This is the 125th anniversary edition of the Haymarket Affair with a brief history of the labor movement. The book highlights those who are buried near the memorial, including the eight. There are biographical sketches for all those who were active in the labor movement from the late nineteenth century onward, as well as those whose lives have been affected by the Haymarket events. This work was inspired by the Adelman tour book and helps to simplify it in that the Rogovin collection

gives those buried in the shadow of the Haymarket martyrs the space in which to have their stories told.

Schaack, Michael J. *Anarchy and Anarchists: A History of the Red Terror and the Social Revolution in America and Europe: Communism, Socialism, and Nihilism in Doctrine and Deed: The Chicago Haymarket Conspiracy and the Detection and Trial of the Conspirators.* **Chicago: F.J. Schulte &, 1889.**
This is the most detailed early work of all the material of the Haymarket Affair. The book details the investigation and trial, the political beliefs of the convicted and the historical importance of the events. Photos of confiscated armaments, banners and other items that were used in the trial are plentiful. This also is another example of telling the story from one side. With the Schaack book, we get the story from the side of the law. There are faithful renderings of the weapons, books and articles that cause one to see the violence of the act, but the book, of course, fails to show the background of the convicted, the mood of the people at that time and the events leading up to the bombing.

Sinclair, Upton. *The Jungle.* **Cambridge, MA: R. Bentley, 1971.**
Sinclair's most famous work, it gives more flesh and bones to the tragedy of unbridled capitalism that survived into the twentieth century. While written a generation after the Haymarket events, it touches the same themes through the "fictional" world of immigrants in Chicago's stockyards. He said, concerning the success of the book, "I aimed for the public's heart and hit it in the stomach." The Food and Drug Administration was an outgrowth of this work that was written as the new century's rallying cry for Socialism. Though it didn't achieve the object for which he intended, it has become a staple of good literature curricula in high schools and colleges.

INDEX

W

Z

About the Author

Joseph Anthony Rulli, a transplanted Hoosier from South Bend, Indiana, began writing fiction shortly after his arrival in his second city. He has one published short story and a play that was performed on stage in the spring of 2016. This is his first published work of nonfiction.

Visit us at
www.historypress.net
....
This title is also available as an e-book